Hearing Voices

The BareBack Anthology

BareBackPress

BareBackPress
Hamilton, Ontario Canada
For enquires visit www.barebackpress.com
For information contact press@barebacklit.com
Cover design and layout by Choi Yunnam.
Compiled and edited by Mike Algera and Peter Jelen

Guts

Bad Day to Write
Nathan Douglas Hansen

Today's a bad day to write.
There's nothing but scratch paper.
Each letter inconsistent,
spelling scars,
and grammar aneurysms.

I'm in a strange house,
in a strange woman.
She talks of food and drink,
wrapped in a comforter
repeating "you, you, you"
as if I have money.

"You're a writer," she says, blinking
cent signs
senseless.
"You've got dough."

I climax a dead man's last breath
Finished,
but not first.
"It comes and goes," I tell her,
lighting a Marlboro as red as her hair.
"It comes and goes,"
I exhale under plumes of my soul.
"Just as I do."

And I put out the fire
in time to start
fucking out another poem
that will cost me
more
than publishing.

Dodgers 2002
Nathan Douglas Hansen

Stuck in an embolism on the 101,
ice cold Lite beer on
burning cold-cocked eye,
and a woman whose name is a season
I can't remember
changes
in the seat beside me.
"Fuck the Dodgers!" she bellows,
beneath a royal blue tube top,
over Korea Town,
banned all but two beautiful mounds of flesh,
pink All-American inside,
blackened with hate.
"Fuck this team and the Italian lot of them!"
she yells, applying an extra inning of
blush,
"They'd play better as guidos back in Brooklyn ..."
lipstick,
"... in a sandlot."
and eye shadow.
"Blind fucks!"

All this under headlight
reflections
in a cracked rear view.
"They're all disinterested,
distracted by Hollywood."
She slipped off her panties.
I swallowed the last of the beer.
I unsheathed my heavy hitter.
She straddled it and stared into
an audience
bumper to bumper,
tits to ass,
hips to dicks,
chrome to shiny chrome,
stripper pole all a-glow.
Homerun.

The blood is flowing;
cock and eye,
bound and blind,
Wonderbread thighs slapping a crescendo.
Parked.

No breaks.
No brakes.
Middle lane.
Split fingered.
Nine minutes, not innings.
"Fuck'n Dodgers," she says,
lighting a Virginia Slim in the still night.
"Can't win 'em all," I say,
lighting a Camel from the butt.
She scoffs and tells me she's a
winner.
She only fucks
winners.
And I remind her that we sat in the bleachers
and she bought the beer.

About the Author:
Nathan Douglas Hansen is a writer and father. He has worn many hats from military to education composing verse in as many places. He balances his poetry between idealism and realism, often focusing on the visceral. Selfishly, he admits his poems are confessional, observational, striving to make him come to grips with his past and present. He rarely shares his words. Hansen's debut novella, "Forget You Must Remember," a fictional autobiography of a stint in a mental hospital, is forthcoming from Jaded Ibis Press. Hansen lives in Arizona.

Fires in Every Window
Mike Algera

Rooftop – Angels weep for the lambs below

13th floor – There are fires in every window

12th floor – A man goes into cardiac arrest

11th floor – A woman has fruits of labour rubbing
between her thighs

10th floor – A woman throws her Vagisil out
the window

9th floor – A child puts the razor's edge to his
scalp to keep lice away

8th floor – A dog in heat leaves a mess on the rug

7th floor – Fire eaters retire with their ice queens

6th floor – A man wearing unzipped trousers climbs
into a summer frock, buttons up for good measure

5th floor – A woman with a head cold and wearing
a winter coat, buttons up for good measure

4th floor – The latest reality show circus crowns
a new Dali Drama

3rd floor – A man spurts Johnny Walker wisdom
at his radio

2nd floor – Angels weep for the lambs above

Lobby – The pillars of guilt hold partitions of silence

Basement – Generators build steam to feed the whole
building

Outside – A homeless man jerks off in the cold for
warmth

Scary Thoughts
Mike Algera

I once pictured my parents
in the act of sex
and when I say act,
it was a freak accident
on Broadway
a chandelier being dropped
from the ceiling, a critic
feigning lead poisoning

the stream of consciousness
jolts from the act of intercourse
to my father waddling
into the bedroom in briefs,
with a hard on
and from there, the satellite
of my mind mercifully
jams into a snow globe complex.

Picture it –
my father. Your father
with an erection. ERECTION.
The bologna has a first name,
it's D-A-D-D-Y.
My father, the Dutchman
probably whittled his wood.
Scary thoughts.
You ask how this could have happened,
well I'm here to say –
yeah. It happened.
Way back when ...

Bob Ray was Prime Minister
the Berlin Wall was up
John Wayne had won an Oscar
the Moody Blues were on tour
the Toronto Blue Jays won
the '92 and '93 World Series

could the ultraviolet ray
revive the apparatus of Frankenstein?

The abandoned auditorium in slides,
ammo from the barrel of a gun
penetrates and festers
in my retinas –
nothing but scattered playbills

pipe organ grinding up dust
from boney esophagus
and malevolent phantom
in abstract form and featureless face ...
scary thoughts.

How could you do this Sue Johanson?
How could you show me the condom
over the banana trick?
You showed me the ins and outs
of a woman, you were the closest
of father figures

but now I have this one 'figure'
stuck in my head.

About the Author:

Mike Algera's first full length poetry book, Old Gods for New is now available in print and as an e-book at www.barebackpress.com. He has also authored two chapbooks, Outskirts and Like Indigenous Tiger. He has been published by Arc Poetry Magazine, BareBack Lit, Hamilton Arts & Letters, Nostrovia Poetry and Cyclamens & Swords Publishing. His favourite themes include dysfunctional families, Oriental mysticism, vigilante justice, love and love in all of the wrong places. He lives in Hamilton Ontario, with his high maintenance dog, Grendel. His home away from home is in digital la-la land, at www.mikealgera.com.

Dirty Knickers
Karina Bush

I think I was awake for all this. He came right out of nothing. A man on the edge of my bed. Licking my dirty knickers. Possessed. Oblivious. He was fully clothed and I was half-naked. So fucking curious. Watching his face. Watching his mouth move. I was excited beyond any state before. I couldn't help myself. My body had taken me over. He didn't look at me once. All of him was in his mouth. Tasting my day. And I could feel it.

He brought them to me clean. Put them back up my legs. They were warm and wet. He told me to wear them again that day. He was German. His voice was fucking perfect. Such beautiful precision on his tongue. Such a hiss. I arched off the bed in a kiss. I wanted to lick it as it spoke. He backed away. He left the room. After he left I could still feel the warmth of him in my knickers, his licking, his breath, evaporating up into me.

All day I was gone. Barely there. In my knickers such a build-up it could have been his tongue sliding about.

That night he was back. Standing beside me. He pulled off my knickers nice and slowly. I was instantly seething. Dilated. I felt prickling all over my arms and legs, like ten men were waiting to get at me. He licked them with more interest that time. And for longer. I couldn't cope. I sat up, made a move towards him and he said no strongly. So I lay back down. I knew my place. And every night he stayed longer and longer. This man was a true connoisseur.

My brain ceased to work alone. Every thought came from my body. Day and night. Uncontrollable. Like the brain is some minor organ I could manage without and my real brain lives in every part of me. Like there is only the body. Like nothing but this exists.

This went on for months. My knickers got so fucking dirty. He couldn't keep them clean. They were

dangerous. Green. And my cunt was green too. And sore.
I could hardly walk. But I didn't care. I wanted the tease
of a fuck more than normality.

They were very heavy now. He'd brought a spoon
that night. He used it to eat from them. Just a bit for him.
Then he spoonfed me all he could. Speaking angry long
German like he hated me. And he licked off the rest nice
and slowly as he scraped a finger and spoon into me, and
I cried in pain and painful orgasm. Then he sucked his
finger clean. It was thick with pus. He left the spoon in
there. And then he put them back on me.

And he never came again.

So I haven't moved. And now my legs are infected.
They are growing really big. And my knickers are stuck to
me, woven through my pubic hair. They have taken root.
I'll lie here until I am black. Until I am given what I have
been forbidden.

About the Author:
Karina Bush is a poet and artist currently living in Ireland. She has recently
published 'Karina Sutra' - some tantric and erotic poems, and 'John's Lottery' - five
stories about johns. All work is available for free download from her website
karinabush.com.

facebook

WARNING: This service may produce delusions of friendship and induce one-way conversations. It may also make you susceptible to cyber bullying and unrelenting harassment. Oh, and it'll totally help the government and corporations to spy on you.

Missis Musician
Rebecca Halton

Emerald eyes
flash to the floor
as those hot heels
Shuffle &
Stomp.

Sparks turn to fire
as she embraces
his blues, his rock,
his jazz

Three steps at a time
hand in hand
up, they
Climb
Climb
Climb

to his apartment
which smelt like
Socks
& Dog.

Burning Branches
Rebecca Halton

We sat and watched
as ember after ember
flickered
from the flame.

Our simple fireworks
danced;
twirling naturally,
leaping into the air,
defying gravity.

Red flashes
and fades to white,
as ashes lifted by wind
momentarily become
confused snowflakes.

About the Author:

Becky Halton is a creative soul, self-taught jewelry maker, avid crafter, devoted writer and full-time student. She recently founded two literary magazines, *Passion: Poetry* (launched September 2013) and *Chick Lit Mag & Indie Press* (launching June 2014). Her plans for the near future include publishing poetry & short-stories, connecting with other writers and planning her wedding!!!Passion: Poetry - www.passionpoetrymag.com

The Difference Between Paint and Ink
Aylssa Cooper

I want to tell him
how ink
doesn't behave like paint.
How ink shows through,
layer after layer,
getting darker
    and darker,
    creating shadows
    out of light;
how ink
can never wash away.

I want to tell him
of the forgiveness
    of paint,
of how my mistakes
can be white washed -
I can lay down new colours
as bright as the sun.

And though a ghost may show through,
a whisper,
I can always add
    another layer,
    and when it dries,
        another,
    one more,
until the canvas is pristine;
as white as snow.

I want to tell him
the difference
between paint
    and ink.
I want to tell him
how paint
can wash away my sins.

The Thorn
Alyssa Cooper

```
She isn't like
other girls;
doesn't taste
or touch
like other girls.
She is sadness built up
in the shape
of a woman;
she is a shard of rage
wedged between
my ribs.
```

About the Author:

Alyssa Cooper was born in Belleville Ontario. A writer with a passion for literary fiction and free verse poetry, her first novel, *Salvation*, was released in 2012. Her first poetry collection, *Cold Breath of Life,* is scheduled to be released in the winter of 2013. She is currently working as a designer in Belleville, where she lives with her vintage typewriters and her personal library.

Ted
Jesse Myner

They made Ted an assistant store manager. I don't know why. Ted refused to write tags for the pallets he put up in the overhead. He claimed dyslexia. Anyone who wanted to know what was up there in the hardware aisle had to take the pallets down and sort through the boxes. It made for quite a lot of work for everyone. Ted made other claims, the most interesting being his ability to heal from wounds within hours. He claimed even the deepest gashes, requiring stitches, he could recover from quickly without any sign of injury. This Ted attributed to having an extra chromosome. The extra chromosome was discovered, he said, by doctors at the Chicago Zoo. He had gone to the zoo for a very special form of testing. This excess of chromosomes also may have affected his diet. Ted said his stomach could only digest raw meat he was unable to eat anything else. Ted was short and round yet said his body fat was at exactly 0%. He said he had been in a major high school football championship game and was headed directly for the NFL, bypassing college, had it not been for a serious injury. I assumed in those years he did not yet have the extra chromosome that allowed for quick healing.

About the Author:

Jesse Myner currently splits his time between Bogotá, Colombia and Alaska, where he goes for the salmon run and to hunt caribou with his Inupiat Eskimo friends. Scheduled for release in Fall 2013 is SLIME LINE, a collection of short stories and overview of Alaskan fish processing. A guide/memoir of his years as a futures prop trader, titled EAT LIKE A BIRD, SHIT LIKE AN ELEPHANT, will follow in Spring 2014.

Chronicles of a Solo Descent
J.M. Medeiros

Driving west to avoid the sun

Eastern echoes in the rear-view

Daylight delaminating

Screen-burned-in-ghost-images

Jagged memories like broken glass

Fuel injected flight

Reservoir on reserve

Burn time minimal

Not enough fuel to get there

Forward on fumes

In the margins of midnight

Cinderella frets over a pumpkin

Armadillos play possum too

Compassion is road-kill

All virtue causes bleeding

Shape of dreams and fancy

Equal enemies inside

Centre-line blind

Contradiction is a direction

When driving in the ditch

Solid white fades to the black-light

Passing lane blocked

Merge to off ramp

Exit to sunrise

Dream awakens dawn

Still Life at Seaside
J.M. Medeiros

I'm older now

But the words are young

Verses with dew still on them. Ringing clear

sounding more saccharine since these in-between

years alone are deeper and grown over with a harder bark

Rolling off my tongue, graceful like the currents of a spring freshet

A creek that begs to be a river, heeding the homeward pleas of ocean salt

Saline lingers, suffused in a single breath as I brush-up close to the memory of your voice

I imagine this, as the beachhead must - embraced in a clutch of tides, caressing the lips of the earth

Scars square the circle of memories. Corners - making it difficult now to return them to me as

recognizable shapes. There are days I manage not to believe every lament has to be

perfectly formed. As it is, there are little enough untainted moments

to fill what's left in a life. From above, this river runs

through both our hearts. And you can see

the earth now, as a

perfect circle

About the Author:

J.M. (John) Medeiros is a poet and writer living in Toronto the area – having travelled to more than 40 countries after (and during) my studies in Urban Planning, Engineering, English and Philosophy – he's lived and worked in Brazil, Bolivia, China, Portugal, Venezuela and in Canada's Arctic regions. His poetry has been published by BareBack Magazine, Dead Beats and will be appearing in Feathertale. His work also appears in the recently published poetry anthology -'Cantos' published in the UK by Dead Beats Literature.

Ever after
Blossom Thom

It never happens like the storybooks.
Princes don't ride up to your door to ask for your hand.
Those frogs that you've kissed
steal your heart to toss against river rocks.
I wish I wasn't as blind as my ambition
but stars don't fall as often as they should.
Instead, I wade among the shallows
collecting the remnants of a giving heart.

Re-acquaintance
Blossom Thom

One day I walked out of our house unadorned
my life complete, golden
like a thread from my bridal garment.
Stepping into the comfort of the street
I welcome the luxury of the unknown.
A blanket of heavy summer blooms ground me.
I walk slowly, until giddy, I stop to laugh with my soul
Full-bodied and loud like a drunk man before the beer drives him to his knees.

About the Author:
Blossom Thom, a writer of poetry and fiction, enjoys the reaction of an audience when presenting her work at readings. Her poetry has appeared in *The Great Black North* (2013), the *Ampersand & la Perluète* (2012), and online in *BareBack Magazine* (2012). Thom presented her prose during the *Lovers and Others* reading (2012) and the *Greene Writers Read* event (2012). Thom's heart led her to Montreal, Quebec where she now makes her home.

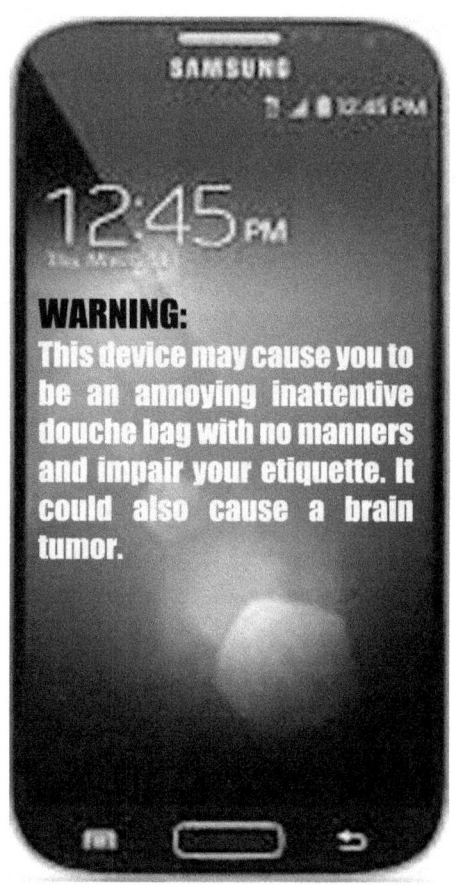

A Black Alley Tail
James Beaton

David clutches the plastic bag in his fist as he walks through the alley. There is the usual graffiti on the walls: *Freedom, Fuck Cops, Fuck Rob Ford, Long Live Mars Bars*. He walks by a dumpster and the smell of garbage catches in his throat.

He has all the supplies: duct tape, rope, garbage bags, and a knife. He opted for the expensive carving knife even though his kitchen drawer is filled with dollar store knives. He has never killed anybody before so he is nervous…and angry.

A few weeks ago his girlfriend Jenny and his best friend Thomas were out for drinks. Thomas said he was okay to drive. He wasn't. Why did Jenny get in the car? Why did Thomas live and Jenny die?

Tonight David is going to make things right.

He is about five minutes away. He wonders what it will be like. Will there be a lot of blood? Will Thomas scream? Not being a seasoned murderer, he has only partially worked out his plan: the killing part. The important part.

A lean black cat emerges from beside the dumpster licking his lips. Despite just having dined on an old chicken drumstick that now rests bedside him, he remains dignified. The cat sits and cleans his paws.

As David passes he hears a voice.

"You don't have any tuna, do you?"

"I'm sorry," he says. He turns around quickly. Seeing nobody, he glances down. The cat blinks his golden eyes and his whiskers stick out like stiff wire. His tail swishes with determination.

"Tuna?"

It isn't as if the cat's mouth moves and the words sound like when a human speaks. For David, it is like having thoughts in your head, like a song playing.

"Is that you?" David asks.

"Yes."

David stares in disbelief, uncertain how to respond. The cat perches impatiently with his two front paws touching.

"I doubt you're really talking. But no. I don't have any tuna," David says. "I'm going to meet a friend."

"With a knife and duct tape? Sounds like a fun night. *Must be a good friend.*"

David looks at the bag. There is no way anybody can see through it. And how is this cat talking? Maybe it's the stress? Or his conscience?

The cat stands confidently and jumps from the grimy pavement to the top of a discarded table.

"Much better. If you think the alley smells where *you* are, you should try being inches from the ground all day." The cat looks over at a wooden chair with a broken back. "Pull up that chair and let's chat a moment."

David's anger has transformed to confusion. His mind is whirring. The situation is so odd but he wants to know what the cat has to say. He grabs the chair and drags it to the table.

"You know. Murder is messy business," the cat says.

"I have to do it. He's a killer."

"I see. What are you going to do with the body? When I kill a bird or mouse, I eat a bit and the leave the rest behind."

"I'm not sure….leave it maybe."

"It'll smell you know. Bodies start to smell pretty fast."

David shifts in his chair.

"Well, I'm not going to *eat* it."

"Of course not."

"Have you ever been to prison?"

"No, and I don't plan to."

"Neither did I. I was out and this man grabbed me and then I was in a cage. You know what they did? They cut off my testicles." The cat pauses. His yellow eyes are as round as full moons. "Then I was taken into a home. It was okay for a while. A guy gave me food and I slept on the couch. But then he got a roommate who hated me so I got dumped here."

"That's terrible."

"If they get you be careful. They like to cut things off."

David bristles at the thought. "I will."

David and the cat listen to nearby traffic, sirens, people laughing in the distance. Then the cat disrupts the moment.

"There's a store at the bottom of this alley. I haven't had a good meal in a while. Do you mind getting me some tuna?"

The cat's eyes narrow and he flicks the tip of his tail.

David sets the bag down next to the cat on the table. He will go buy tuna.

About the Author:

James Beaton lives in Toronto, Canada with his cats who provides endless inspiration and company. He is originally from Cape Breton. He enjoys writing humor, horror and dark fiction. His stories have been featured online with *Absent Willow Review* and *Danse Macabre: DM du Jour*. He has published a story in *After Dark: A Collection of Haunting Tales* through Diversion Press in 2012. Forthcoming is flash fiction with *Leodegraunce* in their print anthology. james.beaton@gmail.com

The Other Side of the Grave
Anne Anderson

Now then. Now then,
Come sit on my knee,
I'm up in heaven watching
a bloody trilogy.

My gravestones been smashed to pieces,
my reputation too.
I just loved all the children.
I fixed it for you and you.

I gave out dazzling badges,
I fixed up all your dreams.
All your parents loved me
as I chewed on cigar seams.

I shook hands with the royals.
I was awarded an O.B.E..
I even had Gary Glitter on the show presenting
with only likkle me!

But the dirty mare got arrested
and removed from all our lives.
A convicted pedophile
who didn't have a wife.

He had lots of unruly hair
all hidden under his cap.
He acted as if he didn't care less,
even in handcuffs he would laugh.

We were a happy family at the B. B. C.
Earthly Jimmy and heavenly me.
Earning extra tickets to get heavenly stripes.
I managed it, I was just about ripe.

Then the Levison enquiry made reporters too frightened to write news,
so poor old Jimmy Saville - was mauled and in death, abused.
I'd still be resting in peace,
if they hadn't have wrote that piece!

People said, that I'd molested them

thirty years ago,
when they were in borstals, prison
or when they were on the dole.

The pot of money at the B.B. C.,
made hundreds say I'd abused my celebrity.
But in the 70s it was fine to fiddle,
even the parents laughed at my wiggle.

When children sat up high on my leg,
everyone knew what kept them pegged.
No one was called a pervert or a fag.
In those days, if you were famous you could sag -
or stand upright, dance wild like Barrymore
You didn't have guards on the stage door.

You could smoke on stage
or drink till dawn.
When having sex with the band
was your one and only calling card.

Ask live people - like Jagger,
the Beatles or even Ken Dodd.
Now then. Now then.
Why the flipping heck not!

If I did wrong on my way upstairs
I need you to know I really cared
I spent my life raising funds for charity
Not spanking schoolgirls over my knee.

Venus Fly Trap
Anne Anderson

His mobile Venus fly trap
took three weeks to conquer my dress
Why me?
I'm just the woman in the supermarket
Buy gravy and ketchup instead

Just cause you're a failing stallion
in a false world of happy families,
although you are very good looking
dip into you're snout bag
Casanova and dream

About the Author:
Anne Anderson is an up and coming challenging poet and novel writer. She has just
released I Hate to Love You under her pen name -Anne Berry and is getting brilliant
reviews. As a final year student at Winchester, she has excelled amongst other and
chosen to represent the university in Vortex. She has also been published in *Splendid
Fred and Praise* too.

Take Heed
Hailli Dee Lilburn

Never doubt that love will arrive at your doorstep

But take heed on how it gets there

If love comes riding a steed with blinded eyes and stomping hooves,

It is noble and proud. A hero, a charmer ready to win your heart

with a handsome face and a flourish of affection.

This love stands in no one's shadow

It demands attention

Prancing like a peacock and snapping like a turtle

Beware the steed

If love comes riding on a mule with slow clip clops and weary breath

It comes looking for aid.

It is sensitive and tender and help it you must

Although this love is full of aches and groans

It strives on out of duty and instinct

Even if it breaks all its bones

Beware the mule

If love arrives by locomotive with coal streaked engineers and steaming whistles

It comes bearing gifts from far off lands,

Exotic fandangled gadgets of amusement and mystery

It is organized, efficient and professional

Spending many hours abroad, driven by wealth and career

Brushing problems under the rug to keep up appearances

A secret keeper

The love in the steam train always carries baggage.

Beware the locomotive.

If love comes by airship with spinning propellers and inventive machinery

 it brings with it the sun, the moon and stars.

Utterly devoted, complimentary and passionate.

It will carry you away on wings of fantasy and impracticality.

A dreamer with big plans that often get lost in the celestial clouds of the heavens.

An artist, eccentric entertainer who rarely sets foot on solid ground.

Beware the airship

If love comes riding the chimera with wild fangs and armoured scales

It comes in strength and carnal magnetism.

Victorious in battle and feared by many a competitor.

Its large appetite can lead to troublesome addictions

Dressed in sour tempers and lies.

Riding the torrential whirlwind, this love meets its end

In gruesome disembowelment.

Beware the Chimera

If love comes on foot with dusty soles and healthy lungs

it comes with no veiled notions

No falsehoods, no pretentions

It has what it needs and is satisfied, practicing longevity, action and moderation.

Slow to build, but needs no renovation

Beware the love that comes on foot

It will be a long lifetime before parting.

Never doubt that love will arrive at your doorstep

But always take heed on how it gets there.

Precious Resources
Halli Dee Lilburn

Dust billows up

Where I sit and sell my crop.

Sifting through harvest stubble and hawk perched telephone poles

I am far

An endurance effort to travel

What keeps you from me? Is it the lure of fossils buried beneath horizon mountains?

Or mountains of steel with their neck ties and profit margins?

Do you have the means? Where a once old horse bent low in the dust bowl watches time

speed past in an iron carriage

And asphalt lays the rust with diesel tanks and lithium batteries.

Could you breeze through the prairie, arching over the curve of the earth?

Hours of fence posts and fields

I am remote

My need a forgotten fuel to you city folk.

When the setting sun glows in your sky blue iris

I am isolated

In the center of your daily bread universe.

About the Author:

Born in Edmonton, AB, Halli Dee Lilburn resides in southern Alberta with her husband and three children and works at the local library. She has work published in Canada's History, Canadian Stories, Poetry Quarterly, Seeding the Snow, Grey Sparrow Journal and SPIRITED ghost stories anthology by Leap Books. Her YA sci-fi novel SHIFTERS is published through Imajin Books. She is a gardener, artist, photographer, seamstress, poet, genealogist, and singer. She can pick up spiders, handle the sight of blood, subdue aggressive dogs, make a mean grilled cheese, and keep her sanity. Most of the time. hallililburn.blogspot.com, twitter@hallilburn.

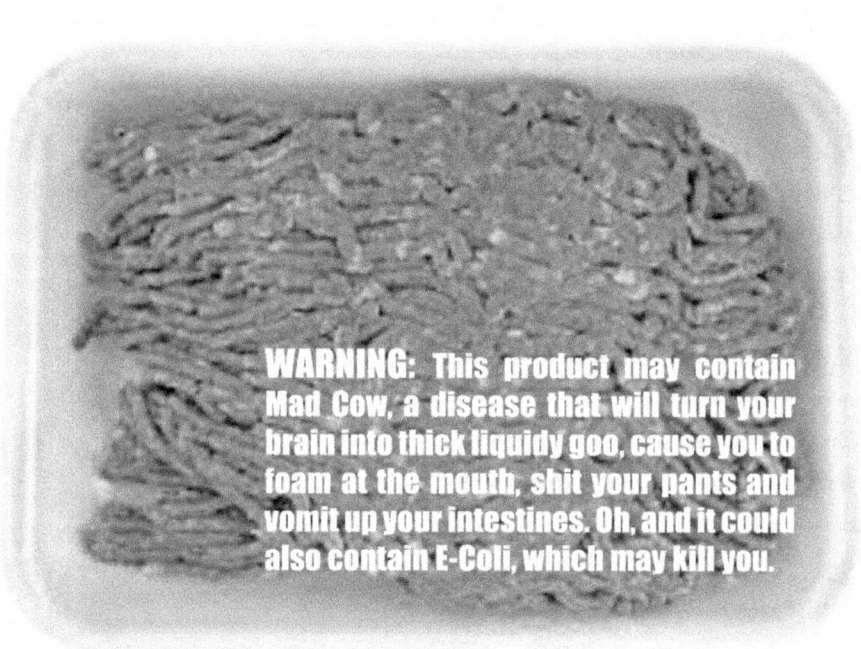

WARNING: This product may contain Mad Cow, a disease that will turn your brain into thick liquidy goo, cause you to foam at the mouth, shit your pants and vomit up your intestines. Oh, and it could also contain E-Coli, which may kill you.

Coveted
Elizabeth Brown

Kate

It was a week since Judas's heart gave out. Waning light bled through Maine clouds like bloody rivers. White caps formed like walls, encapsulated her senses. She watched from the kitchen window overlooking the bay. The boy, two-years old now, dug feverishly for clams, indifferent to the wind that screeched across the earth like a scourge, menacing. The bay was in constant discontent—a foaming wrath, mocking.

The man appeared, drifting off the water like morning fog. Ephemeral, he moved towards the boy. No boat was in sight.

She watched the boy, named Bradley, green-eyed, dark thick curls like his daddy, roguish, crouched down in the mud. She imagined his pudgy fingers finding the holes, digging with fervor. The man was only a few feet away.

It's him.

The boy looked up at his daddy.

Judas … no, dear God. Leave him be!

******

Judas

It was a steamy, Saturday night. Judas was shucking corn when his son wailed. Two days later he'd stop breathing. Titi was in there—arms thin and bare and browned, smeared in female fluids. Judas imagined her laboring, her delicate hands between his wife's legs. Bradley Winifred screeched. Lena sat on the porch swing, combed her doll's hair with a blue comb, mouth parted, waiting.

"He's crying daddy."

"Yes, I hear.

"Why baby crying, Daddy?"

"He is saying hello."

"Oh. We better go, Daddy!"

"Go where?" Judas asked, dazed, as if detached from his corporal body. He was fixated on Titi. It was a new obsession he couldn't quit.

"Go to Mommy and baby, Daddy!"

Judas raked his hand through her hair, wondered how he fathered such a merciful child.

"Yes I suppose we better," he said, indifferently.

Often he had an urge to pick Lena up and hold her. But Kate chastised him, fearing he might hurt her again like the time he swung her and she let go and landed with a sickening thud in the dirt. When she looked up, her mouth was a bloody mess.

"God damn you Judas. Leave her alone."

"I didn't mean it, Kate. You know I feel awful about it, don't you?" he told her that night as they readied for bed.

"She could have died that time," Kate said. "You're too rough with her."

"Okay. I just love her so much...maybe too much." Judas came up behind his wife who was standing in front of the full length mirror. He lifted her nightgown just enough where he could feel her hips. He sought repentance.

"Yes, maybe too much," she said.

He moved his hands up higher. Her chest heaved. The husband lifted her flannel gown up to her breasts, cupped them in his hands; he felt her weaken "Please, now, Judas," she pleaded. He liked it when she became vulnerable, desirous, and he'd pull away. This time he took her and impregnated her. It was the last time.

****

Kate

The mother put the baby to her chest; he latched easily and she calmed at the tug. Titi moved about the room. "It's a hot one," she said, wiping her forehead with the back of her hand. Kate noticed, for the first time, Titi's svelte shape beneath her sheer sundress.

Bradley sucked, and she felt the warm flow seeping out between her legs, the cramping, her breasts aching and swelled, her belly protruding. She considered it, the burden she carried, as Titi flitted about the bedroom, unencumbered and humming. She was youthful, unblemished in mind and body.

"I will go to get them, yes?"

Kate wanted to bask in the quiet, forget the other pieces to her life. "No not yet. Sit down next to me."

So Titi sat down next to her, and rubbed her arm. "Okay Kate. I see."

Unlike her own, Titi's hands were cool and smooth, despite the 100 degree heat. At some point Kate's hands chapped and calloused from years of chores. Titi was young, spared. She tended to Lena in the morning, but spent the rest of her afternoons attending college. She stared at Titi, longingly. She felt a pang of jealousy. Yet, she had no doubt she loved Titi. After all, how often had she defended her when Judas was surly? She observed Judas with Titi when he thought she wasn't looking, caught him reprimanding her for allowing Lena to play in the dirt, or skip her morning nap. Kate attributed the angst to his recent depression. He was a partner in one of the top law firms in Blue Hill but was unexpectedly laid off. Kate never did determine why; each time she tried to ask him about it he became agitated, and one time he put his fist through the door.

******

Judas

The moon was full, shone on the bay, radiant. He waited for her behind the guest house, by a row of tall spindly pines. He grabbed her. She gasped. He held his hand over her mouth. It was time. He was certain she'd succumb once she felt him inside her.

He had been watching her for years now, the way she moved about the house bending to pick up Lena, low cut tops, breasts ripe and newly formed. She saw him looking, smiled at him, and he decided she wanted him too. He knew she was dating a boy. "Why don't you bring your friend by for dinner?"

Kate had said. Foolish Kate, he had thought. He spied on them afterwards, kissing on the porch swing. The boy's hand moved up her leg. Titi pulled it under her skirt. The window was open and he could hear the soft moaning.

Kate surprised him from behind: "What are you looking at Judas?" she asked.

"I heard noises."

"Oh, I see." She parted the curtain and paused there. "Do you like that?"

"What do you mean?"

"I think you know."

She stared at him with loathing and lust. He backed away from the window and from his wife—wary, effeminized.

He had waited a long time for this night. "The moon is full," he whispered. "Just relax. You will like this. I promise."

He pulled her out of view, behind the guest house. He took her down to the grass easy like a quivering bird. "I'm going to take my hand away from your mouth, okay?"

She nodded, yes. He lifted her skirt, spread her legs. Initially, she resisted, but then she was slack, pliable. He was gentle. She let out a quiet sigh.

They fell asleep—bodies entwined. He dreamed of Kate standing over them, aiming a gun. "I knew you liked that," she said and her expression was macabre. And then he felt it— a searing blast to his chest and then blackness.

******

Kate

She knew her son had passed to another realm. But she never believed he was actually gone. The morning she found him, she saw his spirit lift from his body. She never told anyone.

"What is it darling?' she asked. She wondered why he was so still and silent. She bundled him up and put him to her breast. "He's not hungry," she said to Lena when the curious girl asked why her brother's hand was so cold. Lena started crying.

"Quiet down. You'll wake him." She was tired of Lena's questions. And, Titi, lately she'd been arriving to the house an hour late with some excuse. "It's about time we find a new nanny," she said to Judas when he came into the room. He had a strange look on his face.

"Did you hear me? Titi is late again. Damn that girl. The baby is not eating, and I'm exhausted. Lena is upset. What does anyone want from me?"

Lena's sobs intensified. He reached down. "Let me try," he said. Just before handing him to Judas, she watched as a wisp of white mist lifted off of her son, the air became a shroud of fog above her, and she knew he was safe.

Kate never mourned her son. Instead, she became suspicious, convinced Judas was dark, malevolent. She derived solace from Bradley's visits. He sat on the edge of her bed as she slept, or on the kitchen floor when she prepared meals. She talked to him, watched him from afar playing on the water's edge.

She always feared Judas might take him. The wind howled. Kate tried to open the door. Strangely, it was jammed. She hoisted herself up and climbed out the window, she walked down the path, slipping a couple of times on the shale. Her feet bled from barnacles and the sharp edges of rock. She kept going further and further, beyond the shore— the dugout holes in the mud, the blue bucket tipped onto its side. She walked deeper and deeper until the bay gripped her.

******

Lena stood in the doorway looking after her mother. The door was gone, blown off the hinges. The bay shrilled and clamored, perfunctorily. She waited silent, salient like a spirit unsullied.

About the Author:
Elizabeth Brown resides in West Hartford, Connecticut. She has published short story collections and a couple of novellas--psychological fiction and metaphysical visionary genre. Currently she is working on a psychological thriller (novel) and a dystopian novella.

At the Shore
Gary Beck

The sky is darkening,
faces in the sunset light
glow red.
The beach is quieting...
A lone kite soars higher than a gull.
Mother and daughter
dig the last sand castle.
A small boat races home,
urgent to beat the menacing dark.
The glowering pink sky
growls with the weight
of old sol going west.
A cool breeze
blows across the boardwalk,
WPA built in 1937.
Joggers and runners
pound the boards,
startling old ladies
with pink hair
and faded lace shawls.
Then evening slides in.
The sky succumbs to sullen red.
Another casual day ebbs away.
Darkness claims the promenade,
and thoughts of drink, dance and growing lust
propel the tourists to smoke-filled bars,
as the night cycle goes on
to some formless destination,
preparing adornments
before the final funeral.

Vast Seas
Gary Beck

Humanity,
once again adrift
among your wreckage,
I cross stormy passages,
chartless, more fragile
than sailors of old,
whose tiny wooden hopes
made miraculous transit
on unkind seas.
O voyagers who turn back,
I know your fears.
I recognize your hazards,
but foretell your craven end,
unwilling mariners.

About the Author:
Gary Beck has spent most of his life as a theater director. He has published several chapbooks, story collections and novels. His original plays and translations of Moliere, Aristophanes and Sophocles have been produced Off Broadway. His poetry and fiction has appeared in hundreds of literary magazines.

Blessed Rifles
Jeremiah Walton

Rifles blessed by a priest
aim at the weak and hungry
and fire.

Rifles loaded through art of forgetting
the sweeping of shame under the rug
They fire.

Contemporary politics are disgusting
Its rifles are hideous.

The 8th wonder of the world is your body
Your blood is the only flag you should shoulder,
the only flesh to be patriotic of.

You owe no loyalty to your birthplace

You owe no loyalty to repression.

The Morning After
Jeremiah Walton

Electric fault wires, soundgardens of mind
Sparks, roots ringlets wired for elec-stacy
Now is the only concern.
Flowers bud as quickly as they wilt
Gardener is rendered temporarily useless
Electrician divvies up moaning and dead
Into past and present
Their inquiries hitting dial tone
No coffins, only abysmal hovels of rich soil
Fertilized by history of embryonic Self.

About the Author:
Jeremiah Walton graduated high school the spring of 2013, and hit the road hitchhiking the following fall, making his way through every open mic and slam along the way. Jeremiah manages Nostrovia! Poetry, W.I.S.H. Publishing, The Traveling Poet, and is an editor at UndergroundBooks. You can follow his travels and poetry at Gatsby's Abandoned Children. He is author of Gatsby's Abandoned Children and Smile W/ Sparks (of a shotgun shot).

This Grief
Elizabeth Houlton Schofield

There is grief so powerful, that acknowledging it thrusts you into the undertow of the ocean in a fall storm. Legs torn out from beneath, head slamming shingle in one breath-claiming blow, feet first into the abyss, wrenched from the anchor of the shore. It is not falling; it is being hauled into oblivion.

This grief, this bone-aching emptiness only happens once or twice in a life, for who could withstand repeated assaults of this magnitude? Who would want to wake again to the certainty of living?

It is the loss of a child. We are not made to outlive our children; to bury our own babies. The empty palm, forever deserted by tiny fingers, destined to be a hollow well at future greeting.

This grief is the loss of a life-to-be-lived. The nine month child a changeling at the point of birth, switched for one unknown. No longer is she the anticipated, the expected, now she's one whose path is halted or diverted by diagnosis. All the rosy plans of gestation, the musings on ballerinas, engineers or grandchildren are swept aside by appointments, tests, echoing attempts at reassurance.

It is the gravid weight of pregnancy, pulsing with promise, stealthily ended. The lifeline cord of flesh is now a noose. Hint of change, of ending, turns into nagging doubt, unspoken fear. She prays to be wrong. A mother always knows, bargains with the universe that the knowledge is misplaced, certain it is not, but hoping, hopeless.

This monumental grief is the realization that life has no purpose, has never had purpose, that the human condition is one to be suffered until... Until? The void of loneliness in this existence is the format for eternity. Grief unspeakable at the failure of a life lived to deliver any hope or fragment of promise.

It is the ending of a dream, a deep felt wish, and love. When love and dreams are absolute, they are the reason for existence, the prompt for breath, the spark of the heartbeat. If love can render you speechless when it walks into a room, what can it do to you when it walks out?

And yet we love still, and again, and after it has gone with no hope of restoration. We invest our lives in the future of our children, knowing that return is less than guaranteed, never hesitating to take another risk on their behalf.

To love a child, life, a lover is to run into the ocean, each time new-made with insinuated promise, ignoring the warning sign on the lifeguard's tower. There is no living life in certainty, in peace. Life's flame is only coaxed to roaring in a howling gale.

Risk this grief again. Exhilarating, unpredictable, do it again. Take the hand of a child, shiver at a lover's touch, find a purpose in the smiles of others smile upon, and live. No guarantee, just live.

About the Author:

Elizabeth Houlton Schofield's astute observations of everyday life drive her creativity and joy with words. Liz's stories have appeared in the Globe and Mail, and Barebacklit and will be published in Drunk Monkeys in 2013. She won the Honorable Mention at The Surrey International Writer's Festival, 2013, and was published in the Conference Anthology and has been shortlisted for Literary Writes 2013 (Federation of BC Writers), and Room magazine's Reader's Choice Awards 2012.

Dead Eye
Ross McCooey

Dead eye leans
against the rain,

content in Tombstone
before tumult and contest
corral the silence.

Silvers flash, tumble
and he spits stiffly:
the eye is smoking

and legend is spun
by a single action.

Another dollar
for a hollow point -

all in a day's work.

Hallucigenia Magna
Ross McCooey

Cutting mobs blossom
a purity that barters
our dependence.

Bloodtracks vein and thunder
like heroin in nighted lights:

neon and babble
from the maws of
Hallucigenia magna.

Pull it through the crumbling walls
and stare at the blank TV screens.

About the Author:
Ross McCooey lives in Dublin, Ireland. With a strong interest in physics and
biology, his writing attempts to blend scientific fact with poetic observation to create
pieces that resonate with readers on numerous levels.

Elegy for Florence
Damon Ferrell Marbut

Mother brought home
Grandma's shampoo.
It sits around my bottles
and I can't, haven't yet touched them.

Patrick tells me I should.
He is right.

My cousins and I called her Nannie,
she's been dead for months
and her breath still envelops
my memory of her,
how she read silly gossip rags
and watched soaps,
switched me once for aggravating
neighborhood children.
I miss her placid laugh.
Don't know if I miss her.

I can't use her shampoo.

She had an ironing board in her bathroom
and Grandpa is broken
over her. They were quite a pair,
brought food to poor families
in their county, I tried to help
with money after my father passed—
it wasn't enough—
didn't help the way I'd wished.

Wanted to buy my Florence back.

Thought about this in the shower
after work, something that always
kept me from visiting (work),
a shallow excuse,
just trying to say "I love you"
now when now has quietly
passed and all there is left
is apple essence of Nannie
and her near
as I bathe,
like when I was a boy.

Teacher
Damon Ferrell Marbut

I came to your door
because of one note in an Ave Maria

and you said

"It's proper to call someone
before just showing up."

I kept going to class
and encouraging others.
Told a joke or two.

In college we met for a beer
and you said I was suicidal.

Now I look back at the flowers
between me
and your voice.

That note still sings
Most destruction is minor.

About the Author:
Damon Ferrell Marbut is author of the acclaimed coming-of-age novel *Awake in the Mad World* and the collection of poetry, *Little Human Accidents: Chaos Poems From the Brink.* He currently lives in New Orleans, Louisiana. Connect with him at www.facebook.com/DamonFMarbut.

Her Royal Majesty
Neal Whitman

We sit in the doctor's office. Our hands in tight clasp. He sits on the other side of a large desk. He wastes no time. "I have bad news." I hear the words, "breast cancer," but he must be talking to someone else in the room. This could not be Elaine's chart he is holding. In 5 days I drive Elaine to the hospital for surgery. One month later she will start chemotherapy. There is a long list of side effects. Elaine marches into her hair salon. "Matt, give me a buzz cut." "Really," he asks. She tells Matt what's up. In no time, he is sweeping her hair off the floor, into a dustpan, and into the trashcan. She asks, "How much?" "Are you kidding, Elaine, my dear. This one's on the house. Come back in 6 months and let's give you a new doo." I come home from work, walk into the living room, and see a royal princess sitting in Elaine's rattan peacock chair.

About the Author:
Neal Whitman has published over 200 Western form and 400 Japanese form (haiku & tanka) poems. He treasures collaborating with his wife, Elaine, by creating haiga that pair his haiku with her photographs. Also, in recital, they combine his poetry with her Native American flute. Neal and Elaine are volunteers at the Hospice of the Central Coast where Neal just completed a six-week workshop, "In Your Own Words," that used poetry and prose to help people deal with the loss of a loved one.

A Hole in One
Wayne F. Burke

She pulled on my dink as
we sat in the car, the radio
on, the golf course dark;
I watched her white hand stroke.
"My arm is getting tired," she said
and the hand stopped.
I felt like punching her
and ripping off her dress.
"Just a little longer," I begged.
She sighed and the hand moved
up and down and
I shot a wad onto the dash
and onto her hand
which she held up to the moon light
and asked "what do I do with it?"
meaning my cum
and I said "lick it off," or should have said
but did not;
instead, I found a Kleenex
and gave it
to
the dumb cluck.

Last Kiss
Wayne F. Burke

Moving from mouth to mouth
kissing every girl in the bar
their boyfriends stand aside and
stare and one bitch has a fit after
I smack her lips and soon I am
outside and lying on the sidewalk
beneath a tree and listening to
wind rustle through the leaves
and if god has a voice that is it
the soothing shush and rush of
sibilance, the whispered hush and
sudden gust of exhaled breath
calming me but not enough
because later I climbed the side of
a building and broke in through
a third floor window and came to
sitting on a bed in a dark room
and heard the footsteps of a giant
outside the door which flew open
to let a cop in who handcuffed me
so tightly the cuffs stayed on my wrists
for years.

About the Author:
Wayne F. Burke lives in the central Vermont area, USA. He does not ski, hunt, or fish. His poetry has appeared in a variety of publications, on the web and in print. His book of poems WORDS THAT BURN is published by BareBack Press (2013).

Rooftop, Patio, Rain
Denver Jermyn

It isn't time yet
to let the rain win
it comes anyways
selectively on pages
draping imperfect drops
painting impermanent
road maps on the barn board.
So much reading occurs
over others' shoulders
pulling skin tight
next to eyes, lamenting
delayed trains on recently
discovered antique tracks.
Then the apertures shift
blurring the end light.
Deafening forks have
to be defeated
ducking into doorways
dredging salt lakes
and circumnavigating sidewalks.
The piles of molted skin
and cloth grow as
the mirrors slough
each significance.
This time the rivulets may
direct them to the drain
and whatever envelope arrives
should be opened.

growth kinetics
Denver Jermyn

1.
wait

2.
look up
at providence beaming
flat earth expansion crawls
on the surface tension
getting heavy

3.
slowdown
syrup strands of repetition
the cosmos were explored
turning up empty
the exponential is lost

4.
lie back
catch wind of plateaus
disappear stomachs
the five stages of
the grief of power

5.
fall through
walls chafe shapes
in cracked skin

inevitable empty
decisions heaped
at the bottom

About the Author:
Denver Jermyn currently lives, works, and studies in Toronto. His poetry has appeared in Vallum Contemporary Poetry Magazine, Chrysalis Zine, and BareBack Magazine.

WARNING:
This country may
cause you to die
waiting for a doctor.
But you'll probably
get taxed to death
first, so don't worry.

Lincoln's Boys
Harry Posner

Sheets red bleached stink. Bed a concrete altar. Hard as soft. Air hurts lungs. Sunlight scissors through blinds as crack of carbine. You feel-sense the crater, big as cannonball in your guts, or what's left of them. Shear white stretched heat, needles of pain tattooed across the gap.

And where's Elijah? Elijah brother, who's always been…

There there, son, just relax, says Corporal Jamison. *Doctor's on the way from Richmond.*

But…

Don't worry, the Feds won't stop 'im.

Elijah.

Never mind Elijah. He's with Sherman, remember?

Your mind a feast for worms, gorging, delirious, scrabbling crab-like along inside curve of cranium. Exits cloaked. Guarded by swordsmen, and you want to leap out of cot, reverse through tent flap, crawl backwards into powder-smoke-billowed forest, groping blind across Union bodies still warm, fucked by bayonet and bowie, the ignorance of war, moving crabwise back to curl around the cottonwood trunk, exploded shards of musket reassembling themselves, slide back up into nestle of shoulder and arm.

Buck and ball, like blackbirds, whistle back out of your guts, flocking towards the guns of the cooled Confederate carrion, lying like grey-downed mushroom logs amongst the trees fifty yards yonder. The scream of your shot, one by one, rushing back to tunnel through barrel into firing chamber, uncock, untamp, powder and shot disgorged into paper packet, unripped, fingered back into ammo bag.

The healing, the silence before, back creep of men and strategies and fear.

Animals hind back in, upchuck leaves and flesh, birds' melodies warble from end to front. You scrabble rearwards towards camp, dark blues becoming once again fresh from river wash, whole, no hole. Backwards troop on the road, Lincoln's boys, the laughing, camaraderie, songs of the North swallowed by young throats, the memories of Mother and Granny Jens and the sweet breasts of blond haired Annie cupped in your hands.

Her mouth, an orchard.

Apples rise up from wet earth to reattach, grow small and disappear, as you grow young to unplay hoops and untag, deconstruct twig forts, fall on knees to fours, push mouth up for suck of Mama's tit; rocked, rocking, sliding inwards, the dark of her tunnel a drowsy cave, cannon beat of heart echoing in your tiny barely here ears.

And maybe you arrive into the nothing of which you have no words to describe.

Is Corporal Jamison sighing as he slides your eyelids closed, uttering a tired prayer for a fallen soldier? Does he drag the tattered sheet over your head, pull on a pair of white gloves, head back out into the morning mist in time to hear the news that a sniper on the road killed the doctor?

Back in the tent, under the motherly embrace of sheet you lay, breath held forever in the arms of eternity, where none of it happened then. Where there is no then. Never was. Where no clocks tick away, leach away lifetimes, where seeds are always and forever trees, and mountains are never anything but grains of sand. Sifting like mute soldiers through the fingers of eternity.

About the Author:

Harry Posner is a self-published poet and author, whose love of the printed word evolved in a natural progression from short story writing to children's picture books, to poetry, novels, and spoken word performance. He is part of the poetry/percussion duo known as *The Rubber Brothers*, and is a member of the Words Aloud Poetry Collective, as well as the Headwaters Writers Guild, Writers Ink Alton, and the League of Canadian Poets. *Lincoln's Boys* is excerpted from his in-progress collection of flash fiction entitled AND MAYBE YOU FLOAT AWAY.

one-two buckle my shoe
Carl Miller Daniels

you think any of this makes sense?
that some people bloom and prosper, and
other people wilt and die?
that the fruit punch at a party
for an 18-yr-old sex-god beautiful boy
not only contains alcohol,
but tastes really really good?
that the art created
by a van-gogh wannabee
goes unnoticed and unloved
and finally gets thrown
out with left-over home construction
materials?
you think any of this makes sense?
oh come on now. i suppose
you think it makes sense that someone
somewhere is using
a washboard to mash grapes
for dying sheets
for putting on beds
to be slept in
by sexy naked big-dicked teenage boys?
why do sexy naked big-dicked teenage boys
need to sleep on sheets that have been
dyed with grape juice? and why must
those grapes have been mashed on
an old-fashioned washboard?
you think any of this makes sense?
that movie that you saw that
made 3 trillion dollars world-wide
is
just as good as
the one that sputtered
out in the first week,
and no one ever saw again,

until it achieved cult status, that
is, and went on to make
a respectable 8 trillion.
and that first movie,
the one that made 3 trillion,
falls into disfavor, and
when people see it at
drive-ins, they're only
interested in having
sex with the person
that they
brought to the drive-in
because they hoped
to have sex in the car with
that person. does it make
any sense that they go to
a movie and then don't watch it
at all? of course you could
say they just want the privacy
of being alone in a car
at a drive-in, and they got
taught that drive-ins are sexy
places to have sex,
and
when, in one of the cars, the
two sexy big-dicked teenage boys
who are in the front seat of that car
unzip each other's pants and
jerk each other off into their butter-drenched
popcorn napkins
during the most exciting part
of the movie, does it
make any sense that
the two sexy naked big-dicked teenage boys
use popcorn napkins
to catch their jets of cum? no,
not really, but kinda sorta.
listen, you just can't look
for the logic in certain things,

because there is none.
does it make sense that an
asteroid crashed into the earth
and killed all the dinosaurs?
does it make sense that
some people think
the earth is only 6 thousand years old?
when dinosaurs died out millions of
years ago?
summary:
"believing that stuff makes
sense,
just doesn't make sense,"
thinks the sexy naked big-dicked teenage boy
as he lies on his back alone atop his
bed in the middle of the night,
and tugs on his dick
and tugs on his dick
waiting the moment of orgasm
when the cum goes spurting out
of that tiny little pee hole at the
tip of his great-big dick,
and the origin of the universe
is jellied toast on the back
of a sea turtle,
mermaids singing lullabies
at the top of their lungs.

green green green
Carl Miller Daniels

while crunching on a celery stick
with his big white teeth,
the sexy naked big-dicked teenage boy
watched himself in
the big mirror that was mounted
on the back of his bedroom door.
the sexy naked big-dicked teenage boy
looked good,
lean, lithe, sinewy, athletic,
standing in front of that mirror,
crunching away on that celery stick.
in fact,
he looked the pink of health.
his big thick dick was
hard as a rock.
his jaw muscles were tight
and firm and made his
jaws look especially sexy
and rugged
as they worked with his
teeth and tongue and
throat all nicely coordinated
to finish off that
nice crunchy celery stick.
in fact,
the sexy naked big-dicked teenage boy
looked so good
that he took it for granted
that he'd always look this good,
took it for granted that
he'd never get old.
took it for granted that
his big thick dick would
always work this well
and stay this hard

for whatever he wanted
it to stay hard for.
the sexy naked big-dicked teenage boy
stands there crunching the heck
out of that celery stick.
a moment in time.
that, by all rights,
should just
go on
forever.

About the Author:

Carl Miller Daniels lives in the United States. He's not a cowboy, but thinks about them a lot. His poems have appeared in many nice places, including Chiron Review, Citizens for Decent Literature, The Commonline Journal, DNA Magazine, FUCK!, My Favorite Bullet, and Zygote in my Coffee. Daniels has three chapbooks in print. And his first full-length book, Gorilla Architecture, was recently published by Interior Noise Press. His next full-length book, Saline, is in the works, also at Interior Noise Press. Daniels and his partner, Jon (aka "the sweetest man in the world"), have lived together for over 30 years.

Meeting Mister Ruaumoko
Valerie Connor

It's hard to imagine that her fate could be swayed by the choice of a red or a blue dress.

There were the judges to consider, but just as importantly, which would be more pleasing to Mister Ruaumoko? Ultimately, it was Mister Ruaumoko she needed to win over.

Anya took both dresses from the rack and tried them on. Definitely the blue. It matched her eyes exactly.

She'd waited twenty-one years for this. From the day she was born, every aspect of her life had been managed so that she could be on this stage tonight. No detail could be left to chance, however seemingly insignificant.

There was no questioning her destiny from the beginning. Though she was one of five daughters, even as an infant, everyone recognized her special radiance. Her eyes were brighter, her skin more luminous, and her blonde curls really did sparkle like gold.

Anya started on the pageant circuit when she was six months old.

Everyone on her island entered their baby daughters. Now, as one of the seven final contestants for the biggest national title, Anya is obligated to make guest appearances at several of these hokey competitions.

The preschool pageants haven't changed much since she was first on stage. Infants are dressed in six hundred dollar dresses, dripping with ribbons and lace, paraded on stage by beaming parents. Stage mothers bellow at their toddlers because they don't smile long enough at the judges. Backstage, former drag queens demonstrate a perfect hip thrust and shimmy to a group of five-year-olds preparing for the grand finale. In the background, there are always the cries of the tiny contestants who are overtired and hungry.

Sometimes parents wonder if it is really worth the effort. But when Anya or one of the other final contestants arrive, it's like a ray of light has brightened the convention centre. Parents are hopeful, they are reminded why they are devoting so much time and energy into glamming up their little girls.

By the time the girls are six, the competition has become much more intense. Pageants are serious business on the island of Australatica. Professional coaches and stylists are hired at great expense to competing families. It's a huge investment, but the prizes grow with each level of competition. Cars, scholarships, even houses are up for grabs. But at this level, it's still just a rehearsal. Everyone has their eye on the big prize, the national title of Miss Australatica.

By the time the girls are ten, the contest is a nationwide search, with a thousand hopeful contestants. It's a cat fight each year, as girls are eliminated and hopes are dashed.

When they finally reach twenty-one, there are just seven girls left. All the contestants are winners, but only one will get the title and a chance to wear the crown. And only one will be granted an audience with Mister Ruaumoko.

For months now, each element of the final pageant has been televised across the country. It's a national obsession as everyone watches and cheers for their favourite contestant.

Since Australatica is now an island in the South Pacific, it's only natural that the first event would be the Swimsuit Competition. The girls' bodies are nearly identical. Since they were eight years old they have engaged in the same rigorous schedule of daily ballet, weight training and aerobic exercise. Anya doesn't win, but she is not surprised. She knows the pageant organizers need to keep the suspense mounting.

Most Photogenic is the next event. Anya easily wins this one. With her ethereal countenance, there would have been an uproar had this title gone to anyone else.

Penelope wins the Evening Gown competition, and Lily takes the honour for Public Speaking. Anya isn't worried. These are lesser events.

Anya knows that the competition is really between her, and Clarice, her dearest friend. It's funny, since childhood, all the girls were ruthless competitors, biting at each other's backs in the hopes of making it to the next level of pageantry. But once the final seven were chosen, everything changed between them. The girls realized that their days as pageant contestants were coming to an end. Regardless of who wins the big title, all of them will be revered citizens of Australatica. Anya loves all six final contestants, but Clarice is especially close to her heart.

It's almost time for the Diving Competition. Anya can execute a perfect swan dive from a height of thirty feet, but Clarice really looks like bird taking flight when she leaps from the platform. Anya is astonished when she finds Clarice retching in the bathroom outside their dressing room.

"Clarice, what's going on? You're on in five minutes!"

Clarice wipes her mouth with a handful of toilet paper, and slumps back against the wall. Her eyes are glassy and her upper lip is beaded with sweat.

"Anya, I'm so scared," Clarice moans. "I don't know if I can go through with this."

"*Have you lost your mind?* You're a *final* contestant, one of the *Chosen Seven*. There's no backing out now." Anya soaks a towel in cold water and starts to wash Clarice's face. "Everyone in the country is watching us. We have responsibilities."

"I'm terrified of meeting Mister Ruaumoko. What if he doesn't like me?"

"We're *all* nervous about meeting him. He controls everything on this island. " Anya helps Clarice to her feet. "You've worked too hard to give up now. After all our years of training and competing, *no   one* better   deserves   this opportunity."

Clarice glances nervously around. "Sometimes I really wonder about this *opportunity*. Didn't you ever think what it would have been like if *you* were eliminated years ago?"

"Keep your voice down!" Anya hisses. "You never know who is listening. You almost sound blasphemous."

Clarice looks stricken, and Anya tries a kinder approach. "You're just nervous. Let me fix your hair. You don't have much time." She guides the limp Clarice to a dressing table and starts combing her hair. "You know being one of the Chosen Seven is the highest honour a girl can achieve in Australatica.

Clarice wipes her eyes and tries to compose herself. "I'm sorry I fell apart. I know my duties, but our pageant days are almost over. Didn't you ever wonder what it would have been like to have a normal life? Go to a regular school? Date boys?"

In the middle of wrapping a perfect chignon at the base of Clarice's neck, Anya pauses for a moment.

"I suppose dating would have been nice, but you know Mister Ruaumoko wouldn't approve." Anya sighs. "There's no point in wondering about it. We would have been eliminated on the spot if a boy came within ten feet of us."

She spins the stylist's chair around and wraps her arms around Clarice. "It's going to be fine. Tonight we start a whole new chapter of our lives."

Clarice manages a weak smile. "You won't miss your family?"

"Of course I will, but they're going to be so proud. I wouldn't want it any other way."

****

Clarice pulls herself together, and as expected, wins the Diving Competition. There is only one event left, the Talent Competition. This is the big one. Naturally, the Chosen girls are the most beautiful on the island. The Talent Competition is their chance to show their spirit, demonstrate what makes them unique, and worthy of wearing the crown.

Cassandra has a voice like an angel. Ophelia dances more gracefully than a butterfly sailing with the breeze. Roxanne shows she has the heart and strength of a lion with an extraordinary tumbling routine. She flies across the stage, tossing and twirling a baton made of bamboo, kerosene flames licking both ends.

All seven contestants have extraordinary talents, but Anya knows how to reach the hearts and minds of the judges. She glides across the stage wearing the simple blue dress she selected earlier. She chose it not only because it matches her eyes, but it's the exact colour of the ocean that surrounds Australatica. The ocean that simultaneously sustains and terrifies the island's inhabitants.

No one realizes until now that Anya is a poet. In a sweet and clear voice, she recounts the tale familiar to all citizens of Australatica, but she recounts it in her own eloquent style.

> "Once we were not an island.
> Once we were not alone.
> Once, our fathers were arrogant,
> And the earth moved beneath our feet."

There is a collective gasp from the audience. Anya's words bring their history to life. How by the end of the twenty-first century, the geography of their world began to change.

> "Fires, hot beneath the ocean floor.
> Fires burning, rip apart our land.
> Fires raging, consume our people.
> Ancient Volcano, waiting for an answer."

Anya's eyes are blazing now.

> "'Global Warming', cry the Scientists, Heathens!"

Her voice turns venomous.

> "Allah, hear our prayers
> Yaweh, save your people.
> Jesus Christ, show your mercy.
> God in Heaven, deaf to our cries."

Anya pauses, emphasizing the futility of worshiping Gods above the earth. When the plates of the earth rapidly separated and whole societies perished, everyone realized that the real power was *below* the surface of the earth. As Anya finishes, her voice trembles with hope.

> "Look back, sing the prophets
> Look deep in our past,
> Remember Ruaumoko,
> Remember your gift."

All the other contestants finished their talent routines to thunderous applause, but everyone is silent when Anya finishes. There isn't a dry eye in the amphitheater, nor in any home in Australatica watching the live feed. In that instant, Anya knows she has won.

The judges tally the final scores and the all the girls are brought back out on stage. Anya is strategically placed in the centre of the Chosen Seven, as she knew she would be. The girls all hold hands, giggling nervously. No one is surprised when the announcer makes his proclamation.

"The judges have decided! This year's winner of the Grand National Title, Miss Australatica, Queen of the Ocean and Bride of the Volcano God," the announcer pauses, and a drum roll builds, "Miss Anya Anatolia!"

The crowd roars as Anya steps away from the other six and gracefully makes her way to the 30 metre diving platform in the centre of the stage. The pool for the Diving Competition has been removed. She had won, and she would be crowned.

Standing at the base of the ladder, she is draped in flowers and scented oils. She saw her parents in the front row, bursting with pride. Finally, a tiara with a flowing white veil is placed on her head.

Anya climbed to the top of the ladder. The theatre audience cheering evolved into a familiar chant.

Koha, Ruaumoko, a Gift, Ruaumoko.

When she reached the diving platform, she waved, and gave the crowd the benevolent smile they have been waiting for.

The stage floor opened up below her, revealing a pit of flames. She stepped to the edge of the diving platform, raised her arms and executed a perfect swan dive into the welcoming arms of Mister Ruaumoko.

About the Author:

Valerie Connor enjoys writing short stories and her work has been featured in ParentsCanada Magazine and long-listed in the Canadian Writer's Union Contest for Developing Writers. Her work has appeared in on-line publications Barebacklit.com and HalfwayDownTheStairs.com

.:. Flood poems
Robert Swereda

an ignored canvas
justifies your landscape

howling warmth I wouldn`t choose to be
dirt, a historic high anthem for uninhibited
follow the action from a perch
wiring unbraced glimpses
hotbed method come under dispel
surrounding aims for two-prong purpose

wanted sand, different kind of film
gravel: the following year
in your respective hovels shut inside force
plunged into tenor confessions
fell into rebuffed shifts- traditional gatherings
scenarios and ocean neighbours

collect. remind me of being out running into
note pushing pinnacle
long exposure realm of ridicules promises
none of those hands
toward uniformity
where origins gather

Vocabulary, ephemera.
Robert Swereda

faint(ed) : accidentally thrown off balance.

scarcely : causing fatal fall.

gloat : later to become furious.

spitefulness : wanting to safe guard.

crouch(ed) : having to stay where you are.

crawling : problems to deal with.

carven : dressed as and using names of others.

gap : when one refuses to forgive.

clung : to discover schemes of those who pretend to be friends.

torchlight : a life placed in danger.

staircase : confessions that won't be forgotten.

ladder : aiding and abetting a friends crime.

trapdoor : preparing to leave town.

chests : predicting the future.

warnings : caught in lies.

hurried : taken aback.

plung(ed) : a near death experience.

hasten(ed) : signing a contract.

panting : intending to use information received in therapy.

lumbering : pleasing not to expose past events.

skirted : to walk out on important dates.

vast : blurting out to a crowd.

crept : revelation with major consequences.

bent : unlucky in love.

crouch : drowning sorrows in bottles of wine.

waist : tests being done on skeletons.

pinprick : losing virginity.

hiss : distraught.

boom : attempting to land.

sneering : big plans underway.

bound : chance to gain the upper hand.

lowered : feeling guilty about hiding the truth.

chain : an interrupted standoff.

bowed : appearing to tell your whole story.

cavern : facing a shocking sight

filth : evidence in an investigation.

glitter : pretending to suffer from post-partum depression only to have the husband discover your ruse.

plotted : making situations worse by giving into emotion.

defilement : found among possessions of the dead.

blotted : jeopardizing ones' fragile health.

hesitant : reacting to a disturbing sight.

peering : growing more and more suspicious.

haze : declarations of love.

abided : attempt to keep away from.

ceaseless : unexpected admissions that could cost you dearly.

barges : proving self-worth.

jammed : understanding a reason for suffering nightmares.

litters : receiving cryptic messages.

leisurely : opening a new chapter in life.

About the Author:
Robert Swereda is the author of *re: verbs* (BarebackPress), *Signature Move* (forthcoming) and a chapbook *ionlylikeitwhenitrhymes* (100tetes), Robert Swereda has served as a member of the Filling Station collective. He studied creative writing at Capilano University in Vancouver. Other work has been published by The Puritan, ditch, West Coast Line, The Incongruous Quarterly, steel bananas, The Capilano Review, Enpipe Line and Poetry Is Dead.

I Have Learned
Rebecca Rose Taylor

I have learned that if you could bottle patience
Someone would be a millionaire.
I have learned that a smile is someone's biggest asset
And that positive thinking is the key to life.
I have learned that everyone has bad days
But as long as the good days tip the scale, it'll be okay.
I have learned that when people say something that you have heard from the last ten
That you have to be thankful that they care
They weren't around to know that you already heard it.
I have learned that the sky is the limit
You just have to have a long enough arm to reach it.
I have learned that determination will guide you
But you have to have the will to follow through.
I have learned that there are very special people out there
Remember to cherish them; they won't be around forever.
I have learned that there is beauty in everything
Find it and you have a hidden treasure.
I have learned that the weather will do what it wants
And there is nothing you can do about it.
I have learned that money helps
But you shouldn't trade it for happiness, health and those dearest to you.
I have learned that a pair of shoes can be beautiful
And practical all at the same time.
I have learned that you have to think with your head and your heart
And let your hands help you follow through.
I have learned that every day is a gift
And must be treated as such.
I have learned that you make your own decisions
Have your own thoughts
And shouldn't try to be something you're not.
I have learned a lot
And know that I have not mastered all
But that's a good thing
Because that means I am on a journey to learn a lot more.

Eyes of a Bystander
Rebecca Rose Taylor

I can see the path you're taking starting to crumble
like a cliff's edge that you should stay away from.
My desire to shout a warning sticks hard in my chest
wondering how you'd take it.
I'm just a bystander in your life
someone you see every day.
Your life is on the verge of being upside down
like a hurricane rushed through it.
The way you're fighting these fierce winds of change
is so unwise, you've got to give some things time.
Feel sad, be angry, but don't turn to destruction
this is no time for a collision.
Stay on this road and you're going to lose
more than you think you already have.
Maybe you'd say I've never been where you have
you're right but sometimes common sense must prevail.
The answers you need are not found in liquid,
you're using it like a broken life raft.
This time you're going to have to swim with strength
to battle the tumultuous tides in the ocean.

About the Author:

Rebecca Rose Taylor loves writing poetry because of the way it makes her feel. Some of Rebecca's previous poetry publishing credits include: BareBack Lit, Long Story Short and Halcyon. Rebecca is a weekly contributor to the Paradise on Paper Blog. She is an administrative assistant – finance and reception at a senior's home in Quebec's Eastern Townships. Rebecca also enjoys working on her family's farm, reading, knitting, crocheting and quilting.

Tyler
Jay Merill

Tyler's walking up the Aldwych, heading for Lincoln's Inn Fields. He's just come down from Croydon and picked up that it's a good place to be. Feels a bit lost, doesn't know the territory. But he's got his cigs as consolation, has just lit one up, matter of fact. Draws in heavily. Mmm, he needed that. Smoke going down into him till he feels serene. It's a warm moment in spite of the sudden chill. Tyler doesn't seem to have too many of those nowadays. At the Fields he plonks his stuff down on the nearest bench then follows suit. The bench is his island. He's sorry to be on his own in this whole damn universe but there it is.

It seems like an ordinary innocent day of the sort he used to know in the distant past. Before his troubles began. Before he realized what the world was like; lost his job; couldn't pay his bills; got made homeless. If only things could always be this simple and this light. Real life is weighted at the corners, every place and each action heavy as lead, too heavy for one person all alone, to bear. Tyler wishes once again, he had a friend, wishes there was somebody out there to share life's burden. Suddenly he thinks of himself as an outcast. Some tennis players pass him on their way to the courts he'd noticed on his way in. He thinks about how he must look to them sitting here with his backpacks; pictures himself through the eyes of strangers. The goodness of the day dissolves.

Finishing the smoke he thinks about having a nap. Then all at once there's a shout from this loony who's making his way across the grass towards him. 'That's my space,' the fucking loony's going. Tyler squints up into a roaring red face. The guy wants to keep his hair on. Not that he has hair, the guy. And he has gaps where teeth were, if there was ever a time when he did have such things as teeth. Tyler's feeling caustic, he's feeling sardonic. This great hairy bruiser bearing down over his new island home. Only the head is not hairy, rest of him's like an ape. Tyler tries to recall if apes have hairy heads. He doesn't think they do, matter of fact. Of course, he doesn't say anything to the bruiser like, escaped from the zoo, have you? He wants to but isn't about to take the chance. 'Ok, ok,' he tells the nutter. And already he's packing up to leave. Best that way. There's no point arguing.   But, 'Bench number three,' the nut suddenly comes out with. He jerks his head sideways towards a group of billowing trees.

The nut's taken with Tyler it seems, is walking with him down the path, showing him where he can doss down, says his name's Big Bernie. Explains there's another Bernie, further up, bench number nine, and he's a bit on the short side. Bench is fine. Bit damp with a slight urinal smell about the edges but you can't be too fussy. Big-Bernie comes up with a good length of cardboard, clean. 'Thanks mate,' goes Tyler. He's touched. Fellow can't help the way he looks, can't help being a nut. He makes his bed all cumfy on the cardboard, thinks he'll sit up for a bit before turning in. Has his book with him. Toxicity levels in Longshore drift – Tyler was a geography student once, in another life. Hunts for his torch, gets stuck in, lights up a fag. And here he is, quite comfortable like. A home from home. He props himself against the back of the bench, stares up at the sky. Clouds are darkening, turning into night.

Next he hears loud screaming and the sound of running feet. A few figures rush past him in the dusk. Big Bernie's coming over. Been a stabbing, Bench number five. They'll be pulled in for questioning. There's something trickling down his face, Tyler sees. Looks like blood.

'We gotta get out,' Big Bernie says.

In Tyler's heart fear is quenched by jubilation. He's found a friend.

They get their stuff together and set off.

About the Author:
Jay is the winner of the Salt Short Story Prize with her story 'As Birds Fly'. Her two recent short story collections God of the Pigeons and Astral Bodies (both Salt), were nominated for the Frank O'Connor Award and Edge Hill Prize. She is currently working on 'Trev's Friends', a mini series of short stories about the homeless published in The Big Issue Online and is also writing a novel assisted by an award from Arts Council England. Since 2011 Jay has been Writer in Residence at Women in Publishing.

Lives Like Lost Rembrandts
Frank Grigonis

hanging on some forgotten wall

in the last gallery on Earth

which no one visits

while the misshapen faces

of the multitudes

cheer for highly-

televised monsters

who lie for the votes

of the hard working poor

and then when elected

feed only the fat wolves

drooling outside

their thin doors

as the last poets

in the world

die quietly

in tiny rooms

while spinning webs of words

lovely enough to make old Poe

put down his last bottle

and cry

Lives like lost Rembrandts

like the tired, old women

who feed and fix

abandoned cats
from their own parched purses
to no applause
while the slim-souled multitudes
cheer for millionaire athletes
who murder mans' best friends
for laughs

Yet there are lives
like the canvasses
of undiscovered Rembrandts
painted in mostly dark hues
with only small patches
of light
but what little there is
shines blindingly bright

not the official story
Frank Grigonis

met her at the Crazy Horse

said she was Puerto Rican

to me she looked like

one of the Tahitian girls from

MUTINY ON THE BOUNTY

long black hair

longer brown legs

eyes wide with wonder

ass just fat enough

to inspire an army

of rappers

after a few drinks she talked about

her daughter

911 and

how she distrusts the government

then she asked about me so I

told her I was a high school

teacher of literature

which here in America

is about as profitable

and at least as ridiculous as

selling popsicles from an ice cream truck

to detainees in a forced labor camp

in Siberia

but she gave me her number and

three days later I left a message

she didn't return the call

so when I saw her at the club again

a few days after that and she asked me

why I didn't call

I knew there was something wrong with

my perception of the situation, her

or her phone

I called a few more times

over the following weeks

but she never called back and

even if I ask her about it and she

spouts off some official story

I'll never know for certain

what really happened

just like

911

About the Author:
Frank Grigonis teaches high school English. He's also working on a novel which he's been trying to finish for far too long now. He can be reached at fehu9@netzero.net or friended on Facebook.

WARNING: This product contains formaldehyde, a carcinogen used in the preservation of dead bodies. Formaldehyde may cause cancer, brain damage, and if smoked a false sense of well being. On the upside, formaldehyde keeps your Wonder Bread fresh for a month.

What Is It?
Tim Loperfido

So, when I was ten years old there was a weekend that I spent at his house while Mom was away. I had always enjoyed spending time at his house. I liked the pull out bed and staying up late watching television while he snored asleep in his reclining chair. He had a drawer full of snacks that I would always dig into whenever I was over. There was always a whole bag of pretzels waiting for me. Once or twice a week he'd have a woman come over to stock up his fridge and snack drawers — she'd also clean up around the house.

On top of his bad knee, which didn't really become a major problem until later in his life, he had problems with his feet and ankles. He couldn't walk much and spent most of his time sitting at home. Mom used to say that things changed after Grandma passed. He used to leave the house every morning for coffee, but began going less and less. He blamed it on his legs, but that never stopped him before.

So that night; I was sitting on the couch watching the television, we were watching an old western. My grandfather was sitting in his chair and he said in a curious voice, "Did you hear that, Billy?"

"Hear what, Grandpa?"

"I think I heard a noise upstairs. I've been hearing that damned noise all week. Sounds like some kind of scratching."

I remember quickly becoming afraid when he mentioned the upstairs. To that point in time I had never been up there and had always been scared of the stairwell. When I'd walk down the hallway to the bathroom I would never look towards the end. That's where the stairwell was, and it seemed like it led up to an eternity of darkness.

A few years after buying the house my grandfather and a friend of his added the upstairs completely on their own. They built the stairwell, which led to a small bedroom with a bathroom as well. He'd often say that one of his biggest regrets was never putting a shower up there. It was a small house with only one bedroom, living area, kitchen and bathroom on the main floor.

"I don't hear it. Grandpa?" I said.

"What is it?"

"When's the last time you went upstairs?"

"Shoot Billy, it's been a long time. Probably a few years. I just can't make it up those stairs anymore."

"Oh. Grandpa, can I have a snack?"

"Go look in the drawer, and bring me some pistachios while you're at it."

So, I went to get myself some pretzels, a little ginger ale brought him back the pistachios too, and when I sat back down on the couch he said it again.

"There it is again damn it!"

I didn't respond. I used to hate when quietness would be broken by hollering. It made me feel uneasy, like something else needed to accompany the loud noise.

"It's probably some kind of animal. Billy, I want you to go upstairs and check on that noise for me," he said.

"But Grandpa, I don't hear anything," I said to him. And I really didn't hear a sound. The fact that he heard something and I didn't made me feel even more unsettled.

"It's up there, and I'm tired of it. Get up now," he said.

"I don't know, it's scary up there."

"Scary! Gimme a break, what are you talking about?"

He looked at me quizzically, like a dog that tilts his head in confusion.

"Now do what I'm telling you. I'll go stand at the bottom of the stairs while you head up and you just tell me what's there. Like I said, it's probably just a damned animal."

I hesitated for a moment, then shoveled a huge scoop of pretzels into my mouth, and another into my pants pocket. I helped him out of his chair and we walked towards the hallway. When we got to the stairwell he flipped the light switch that was on the wall above the handrail. The light came on from a bulb hanging high on the ceiling above the stairs — barely did its job. He put his foot on the first step, used the railing to hold himself and said, "Go on."

As I ascended the stairs I noticed they were steep, just like my mother had always said — it was like climbing a ladder. Each step made a creaky noise and the hard wood was full of dust.

When I got to the top of the stairs and looked back down towards him, he said, "There's a switch next to the window, there at the top."

I felt along the wall, past the closed window, and found the switch. I was afraid of what I might see when the light came on, but was feeling reassured with my grandfather in close proximity.

As the light came on I felt a wave of calmness break over me as nothing sinister was revealed.

"I don't see anything," I said.

"Go Billy, take a look around. If there's a mouse up there I'll need you to set some traps," he said.

I walked the small hallway which led right into the bedroom. There was no door, the entire upstairs was connected as one. I noticed a dusty old rocking chair next to the closet at the end of the hall; it looked like it would fall to pieces if anyone sat on it — thinking back, I remember it being the perfect size to sit in. Anyway, I noticed how low the ceiling was, and how it took the natural shape of the roof. Near one side of the bedroom the ceiling was very low, and it rose up diagonally toward the other side. Past the closet on my left was the old bed my grandparents had slept on. There was a night table on each side, both with their own separate lamp. One night table had a pile of books, the other an old picture and clock. There was a big dresser adjacent to the beds. On top of the dresser there was large vanity mirror. When I looked in the mirror it had a fun house effect and reflected more of the floor than my actual body. I noticed the old roll out carpet beneath my feet that probably hadn't seen light in quite some time. I realized then that the woman who did the cleaning was either instructed not to go up the stairs, or had been lying about doing so.

I went into the bathroom and saw nothing. Another vanity mirror, pink tiles along the floor and walls. There was a window that looked out onto the back yard and neighbor's house. I walked back towards the stairs.

I said to him, "Grandpa, I don't see it. Can I come down now?"

"Now wait a minute, I think I heard it again while you were walking around. We need to look very closely, if there's a mouse or rodent up there I don't want it making its way down here, especially not into the snack drawer. Now go over near the bed and tell me what you see," he spoke loudly up the stairs, but he didn't have to. The house was so still and quiet that he could speak in a normal voice and I could hear him from anywhere upstairs.

I walked to the bed and sat on it.

"Okay now what?" I said towards the stairwell.

"Tell me what's on the night stand," he said.

"What's on the night stand?" I asked.

"Just follow my instructions, we cannot miss any corner or crevice!"

"Okay, um, there's a lamp."

"Specific Billy, I don't have all day. Tell me what's on the night stand."

"Sorry. There's a picture, an old pic—"

"No! The other night stand!"

"Oh, okay, Grandpa you don't have to yell, I can hear you fine! There's a pile of books and a small lamp, it's a lamp like I've never seen, with a strange shade. It looks like it's made out of some strange paper, but what's this have to do wit—"

"What are the books? Read the titles!"

The books had a smell I never knew existed. The pages were yellow, almost brown, and when I opened them they each had their own sound of the binding bending.

"The Trial, Catcher in the Rye and a few others," I said.

"I don't know those books! Go to the dresser!"

I went to the dresser. His shouting was bothering me.

"Okay."

"What's on top of the dresser?"

"There's an old brush, it's metal and has a design carved into the back, it's heavy. There's a small mirror that you can pick up too. It matches the brush."

"What else?"

"There's a small black box. It has four little legs."

I opened the box.

"Wow, Grandpa there's diamonds in here!"

"Don't open that box! Put it back!"

But I didn't put it back immediately. I looked inside at each piece of jewelry. There was a pearl necklace along with earrings, necklaces, brooches, and bracelets, all mixed together in this tiny box lined with a soft red fabric. When I closed the box I noticed that the top of the dresser was a big piece of glass, and being held under the glass were old photographs. There were images of the same young couple in all of them, and some of them had different people that showed up in various ones as well.

"Now what? Can I come down now?"

"Open the dresser drawers! Look out for a mouse!"

I opened the drawers and there was nothing but clothes. Piles of folded up clothes.

"It's just clothes Grandpa, it's all clothes."

"Describe them to me!"

"There's sweaters, and pants, they all look funny. There's some holes in these clothes. There's a pink sweater, a furry one, there are a couple of black belts at the bottom, and there's a green sweater. The green one has no holes, it's the softest." I held the sweaters up to the vanity mirror to see both sides.

"The green one! Okay put those things back!"

"I can come down now?"

"Wait a minute."

And I noticed he didn't shout. I could hear him mumbling something to himself, but I didn't know what. I heard a few cracks of what sounded like the pistachio nuts followed by chewing. I just stood there and looked around at the room, I walked back to the bathroom and looked out the window onto the backyard and got frightened because it was so dark out. I started trying to avoid the mirrors because the silence was eating at me, and the sight of myself was startling. I preferred to hear his voice while I was up there alone, even if he was yelling.

"Billy! Are you in the bathroom?"

"Yes."

"What's in there? Describe it!"

"It's just a normal bathroom. It looks old though. The tiles are all pink, and some of them are broken. There's another big mirror in here. There's a cup on the sink. Grandpa, can I please come down now? There's no mouse up here, there's nothing. It's just a bunch of old things. Old books, old clothes, old pictures. I just want to come downstairs."

"Wait! Now Bill, two more things, just two more things and you can come down and we'll watch television. I want you to go to the nightstand with the picture!"

"Okay I'm there, now what?"

"Describe the photograph to me, Billy."

"It's a picture of a young lady, but it looks like it might be a painting. I can't tell. It's small. She has red hair and is wearing a pink sweater. Red, curly hair. Is this Grandma?"

"Tell me more!"

"She has a gold necklace on, with a cross on it. Her face looks smooth and soft, her cheeks are rosy, and she's smiling. That's it."

"One last thing Billy, just one last thing. I want you to go to the closet, go to the closet and open it."

I tried to lower my voice and speak softly in hopes that he'd do the same.

"I'm at the closet."

"Open it!"

"It's just more clothes on hangers. There's three or four fur coats in here, a few hats, one with a feather, some shirts that are real shiny and smooth, there's a lot of shoes at the bottom, ladies shoes."

"Billy, there should be a trunk at the bottom behind the shoes I need you to look inside there and tell me what you see, that's the last thing!"

The trunk was heavy as I slid it past the shoes knocking them all over the place. It was black and had a big latch on it with a lock, but it wasn't locked, it was ready to be opened.

"I found the trunk here," I said.

"Open it!"

I was afraid and I was tired of describing everything. I was just so tired of it all. I didn't even want to watch television anymore, I just wanted to go to sleep. I wanted to go home. I didn't want to be there. I wanted my mother.

"Did you open it?" He said.

"Grandpa, what's in this trunk?"

"Just open it, and tell me what you see in there! Describe it!"

So, I put my hand on the latch to lift and open it, but I didn't right away — not at first.

"Billy?"

"I'm trying, it's stuck." I lied.

"Put some muscle into it!"

I took a very deep breath and I could feel my heart racing. I had my arm extended on the latch, ready to lift, but then I remembered I still had some pretzels left. So I grabbed the entire pocket's worth of pretzels and shoved them into my mouth. My cheeks were completely full, the salt was scratching the sides of my mouth and tongue, I sucked them hard and breathed in hard through my nose. I started to chomp on them, but it was rough because all the saliva in my mouth had been sucked dry. Pretzel dust began flying from my mouth all over the closet. Tiny particles of the salty snack. And he didn't give me much time.

"Billy! Come on now, did you get it open?"

I didn't think for just one moment, because that's all I needed, and I lifted it open.

I tried to yell to him, but he couldn't hear me, my mouth was too damn dry and I couldn't swallow the giant ball of pretzel mush that was pinning my tongue down.

"Grandpa!"

"Billy? What is it?"

"Grandpa!"

"What is it! What is it!"

I forced it down my throat, and could feel it stuck in my chest as I screamed to him with all the energy and confusion a tired ten-year-old boy could muster up, "There's nothing! There's nothing up here!"

About the Author:

Tim Loperfido is a New Jersey native who currently resides in San Diego, CA. He enjoys working on short stories, poetry, and screenplays. He is presently studying English at SDSU and nearing completion on his first novel.

9-5
Akeem Akinniyi

To de-spirit a divorce of the divine marriage
of body and soul
I wake up to the sun of everyday into another's vision,
a slave to fortune.

… and I seem to be a castaway.

The sands of time
drift away before my eyes.
I age prematurely
in the alarm clock's noise that ropes 9-5 around my neck.

… and the cockcrow is now an alien sound.

I make a snack of my tomorrow without grudge.
I am not even a shadow of myself but another's.
In snatches, I admire the potentials in my leftover ideas.
9-5 is fool's gold to gifted hands.

… and 9-5 is slow suicide.

To put a light on my name & face
after nature must have separated the chaff from the grains:
given to earth what belongs to earth
given to air what belongs to air.
I dissolve into Time.

… and the mercury of imagination beckons.

With a finger of pen on the land of paper
I gather the sands of time.
I marry my name & face to my story.
What you call history.

Woo-man
Akeem Akinniyi

Like ice,
I freeze, melt in your eyes.
Gather me up in your arms,
my head resting on your chest,
I'll play the child with your nipples.

Like a river lies,
lie on the bed as I rise,
the one-eyed snake between my thighs
has heard the tunes
from the snake charmer between yours.

Fear not, my dear,
it gives no venom but the juice of juices.

About the Author:
Akeem Akinniyi holds a B.A. English Studies from Obafemi Awolowo University, Ile-Ife, Nigeria and works as a copywriter. His poems have appeared in several publications including Saraba Magazine, The Kalahari Review, Ife Poetry Portal, Bareback Lit among other online portals. His honours include a participation in the 1st Nigeria/Korea Poetry Festival 2011 where his entry From Here to There is the title of the anthology.

Day of Reckoning
Jean Jones

Day of reckoning
n
a time when the effects of one's past mistakes or misdeeds catch up with one
Collins English Dictionary – Complete and Unabridged © HarperCollins

Matthew 25:31-46 – The Parable of the Judgment
Summary
In this Parable of the Judgment Jesus' transforms the timeof waiting for the
Son of Man from useless idleness
to the important and unselfconscious care of the neighbor in need.

The judgment will come not as you expected, but it will come.
This day of reckoning, depending on where you stand, will be as
"the day of jubilee"
was for when the slaves were freed,
and the gnashing of teeth of the slave owners when all their
possessions were taken away.
Armies will come and destroy and great joy and sorrow will follow.
God judges with armies.
The Pope may not have any divisions, but God does.
There will be "weeping and gnashing of teeth." There will be
happiness unparalleled.
Those set free will jump for joy.
Those judged and found wanting will be in tears. When is this
coming? Soon. What does that mean? Soon?
Soon. Very soon, the "first fruits," such as Jesus, will multiply.
People will be judged. People will rejoice. People will be put to
shame. Soon.

What is Violence?
Jean Jones

Violence is a forest fire.
All it takes
is a spark,
and with the right ingredients,
it takes on a life of its own,
and it spreads. Eventually,
it burns itself out
or is fought out with fire
and other techniques.
The same with evil and desire to me.

About the Author:

Jean Arthur Jones is an award-winning American poet and an editor. Jean lives in Wilmington, North Carolina near the Cape Fear River. Jean has seen many of his poems published in various journals and books.

WARNING:
This product contains trace amounts of mercury and should not be consumed more than once a month. But if you're trying to give yourself cancer and you want your baby to have birth defects, go ahead and eat it as much as you want.

Second Chances
Carrie Martin

Driving through the desolate plains of Manitoba, Jack sees a woman at the side of the road, waving at him to stop. He slows down, considering the money in the trunk of his car. He should keep going, trust no-one. But she looks desperate, helpless... he pulls over.

"Thanks for stopping," she says through the open window, large travel-bag behind her. "Don't suppose you could take me to the next town?"

"What you doin' out here by yourself?"

"Long story. Please. I can pay you."

He cuts the engine and takes the Chevy's key. "Don't need payin'. Get in. Leave your bag, I'll put it in the trunk."

She slides into the passenger seat, flashing a smile that makes him squirm to be near a woman after all these years. He rushes outside to retrieve her bag, opens the trunk—feels the muzzle of a gun hard against his skull, hears the click of the hammer being drawn.

"What's in the briefcase, granddad?" demands a gravelly male voice.

Jack tenses, furious. "Ain't none of your goddamn business. Now get your gun ou—"

Before he can finish, the gun cracks him on the skull with a force that knocks him to the ground, unconscious.

When he comes to, he's alone in the middle of the prairies, collar of his shirt soaked in blood; car, keys, briefcase of hundred-dollar bills—his whole future—gone.

He sits at the side of the road, stunned, shaking, fuming. Twenty-two years behind bars. Hadn't he suffered enough for what he did? That money was everything he had to turn his life around, start again. What will he do now?

A farmer's truck approaches, and he hitches a ride to the nearest town. He roams the sparse, small-town streets, struggling with the options he has left.

Then, like a prayer answered, he comes across his Chevy hoisted inside a garage, new tire being fitted. The thieving couple aren't there, but he reckons the briefcase is with them, wherever they are. He's got to act fast.

He waits until the car lowers to the ground and the mechanic enters his office. Then he darts across the road into the garage, steals a tire-iron, and wedges himself behind the passenger-seats of his car.

Nobody sees him, and when the couple drive far into the rolling grasslands, he takes his chance. He springs up behind the driver's seat and wraps the tire-iron tight around the man's neck. The car veers right, rips through a field of corn, back towards the road — straight into a telephone pole.

Jack loses his grip, and smacks into the seat. The couple fly through the windscreen — shredded — and hit the road.

Jack stumbles out the wreck, finds the tire-iron amid the rubble, hovers over the bleeding man.

"I ain't no granddad," he says, then bashes his skull in.

The woman is already dead, eyes empty.

Jack takes the briefcase from the gaping trunk, and limps down the open road to start his life again.

About the Author:
Carrie Martin is a graduate of the Institute of Children's Literature, and a writer of quirky and dark from children to adults. British and Canadian bred, she now resides in Tillsonburg, Ontario with her husband, daughter and two wee pets. Her stories have appeared in anthologies by Knowonder!, Mocha Memoirs Press, Source Point Press, Forgotten Tomb Press, Dark Moon Books, and now, proudly, with Bare Back Magazine. Read more at carriemartin.ca

never enough
Linda M. Carte

i bled you a river of flame
equivalent to that of a star
but because it wasn't equal
to the sun it wasn't
enough to appease you
your appetite voracious enough to
burn holes in anyone's galaxy,
and i strove so hard to make you smile
no matter what i did it wasn't good
enough to cut through the pomegranate
melancholy you insisted holding
closer than me, your love;
embracing the void you never spoke
a living personification of winter
so cold that the ice finally chilled me past
the point of return, and i couldn't ever
remain by your side as the bride
of despair so i burned the bridges that
connected our hearts in harmony —
because the love we once shared just turned
to discord, there wasn't enough glue to
hold us together not even the stars
could reconstruct the orange peeled promenade
of hopes and dreams and aspirations we
had once shared before your depression just
pushed us apart; we ended far before
we began, we traversed a path
uselessly unaware of how little either of us would
gain from this venture we partook of.

let me drink you
Linda M. Carte

you told me that you cared
then you walked away
even when i begged you not to
told me it was better this
way, for my heart to
be shattered
like the glass of your winter eyes
cold and blue
distant as the sea;
you used all those rocks to keep me
out, i tried to claw them down
and away so i could get to the
heart of you,
but you always shoved me aside
as if i couldn't understand
what it was like to
be a monster—
have you not seen my fangs
is it because i'm beautiful you think i
only know the confines of
princess-hood?
let me drink your blood i'll tell you
stories of old that would
make your body break into all the
sea figures of shell
you raked against my heart in an attempt
to salt my wounds
ancient and bleeding.

About the Author:
Linda M. Crate is a Pennsylvanian native whose writings have been observed in many publications both online and in print, and whose novel *Amethyst Epiphany* is forthcoming from Assent Publishing.

The Locked Out
Daniel Perry

There were two locks: bolt and latch. From the street he turned his key, clunking the bolt, but when he pulled the door it didn't open. It was nine o'clock, Saturday morning, and his love slept heavily inside the apartment above the shop. Her shift at the hospital had ended at four a.m., while he, finished work for the week, was asleep at a friend's house after drinking beer until the wee hours. It had begun raining around midnight and as neither he nor the friend owned an umbrella, he'd chosen the couch instead of walking home, texting her saying he would return in the morning. When she had entered, tired and presumably drenched, she must have thought nothing of sliding the latch across.

A call would wake her most gently, so he dialed from his Blackberry, but her voicemail answered before any rings – her phone was off, or silenced. He texted and then he sent a short email, hoping one or the other would trigger a different sound. When neither received a response he sipped coffee from his paper cup and frowned. The rain was still falling, and overnight the wind had picked up. His wet T-shirt clung to him and his feet squished in his sneakers' decaying soles.

Knocking would make next to no noise, as the door was a metal framed piece of oft-graffitied frosted glass. Tapping it with a key or a coin was louder, and he tried it but still she didn't come down the stairs. The push-button buzzer never had worked, and when he needed in his habit was to pull and push the handle rapidly so that the door banged on the jamb. But the thundering would be hell to awake to, especially after working so late. He heard a click and looked down to where the cat's silhouette inside put two clawed paws on the glass and stretched before it lay down. *A dog would bark*, he thought. He exhaled and gripped the handle and banged, and waited. Nothing. He looked down at the animal's vague outline and tried to commune with it: *Go get her*, he willed and then said, lowering himself into a squat before the door, which drew a strange look from the shop owner who had come to investigate. *You can sit in my store*, he said, but the locked out declined, saying, *She'll just be a minute. I'll try again.* The shop owner smiled and returned to his counter, his door chime jingling behind him.

On the wet street a car hissed as it passed, masking the locked out's exhalation as he shook the door, trying to make enough noise without sounding desperate, or violent, or drunk – which he wasn't, and hadn't been the night before. But maybe he should have gotten soaked in the dark, the way she must have during her walk home. Maybe when he texted to say he was staying out he dashed her dream of peeling off their wet clothes with teeth chattering and stepping into a hot shower, up too late but being so together and then crawling into bed like they had in university after too-loud music and shawarma when the bars closed. Maybe she had latched the door on purpose.

He began walking down the street, composing another text: *At the library, call me when you wake up.* From the shelf he chose a dog-eared copy of *The Lottery* and he sat at a central table reading its first story, "The Intoxicated." He looked repeatedly at the Blackberry, set to silent, and he waited for its little red light to blink.

He wondered when the rain would stop.

About the Author:
Daniel Perry's stories have been shortlisted for the Carter V. Cooper Short Fiction Prize and have been published in more than 20 Canadian print and online magazines, including The Dalhousie Review, Exile Literary Quarterly, Maple Tree Literary Supplement, and Little Fiction, as well as the Stone Skin Press anthology The Lion and the Aardvark. He lives in Toronto, and on Twitter @danielperrysays.

Car: For Sale
Scott H. Urban

Like the oldest member of the pack,
cast out because he can no longer keep up,
it sits alone in the last row of the parking lot.

Mocked and reviled like toothless Grandpappy
on the slave auction block, its model year
belies claims of little wear and low mileage.

So too have we abandoned the passion
we birthed, neither claiming our off-spring:
a sickly babe on a craggy Spartan hillside.

I've considered jimmying open the trunk
in the middle of the night and dumping you inside—
an unexpected accessory for the next new owner.

nameless
Scott H. Urban

i don't have a name
for whatever it is
that forages unseen
with needling claws
through the sour scraps
at the midnight bottom
of the dumpster

but it's the same thing
that rustles against
the inside of my chest
whenever i
see you

About the Author:
After a lengthy sojourn on North Carolina's Cape Fear Coast, Scott Urban relocated
to the mist-shrouded forests of southeastern Ohio in 2011. His most recent poetry
collection is God's Will (Mad Rush Books, 2013); previous collections include
Alight (Shakin' Outta My Heart Press, 2009), Skull-Job and Night's Voice (Hatchet-
Job Press, 1999 and 1998). With Bruce Whealton, he co-authored the vampire-
themed Puncture Wounds (Word Salad Press, 2009). He teaches composition at a
local college and lives in an Amish farmhouse that isn't haunted -- yet.

Pro Life
Donna Hawks

To my Dead Baby,

Mommy is glad she had you sucked out of her womb,
let you go like a plop of shit into the toilet.

She smiled when she saw you fall into that bag of medical waste.
A wave of relief rippled through her.

Now she has another chance,
a chance to have a new baby grow inside her.
A beautiful baby,
that won't shame her when she strolls it around the park.

Pro Choice
Donna Hawks

To my second Dead Baby,

I'm glad you're dead too.

I'm elated no one will use you for research,
You will not cure Michael J. Fox

You will not take a breath,
Eat, sleep, piss, fuck, shit.

You will not become tainted,
You will remain perfect,

in the absence of life.

About the Author:
Donna Hawks is an angry lesbian who works at a 7Eleven. She writes poetry to cope with her pathetic existence. You can follow her rants on twitter @fknbitchriotgrrl2077.

A Melpaso Production
Andrew J. Simpson

At one thirty in the morning I wound up on a couch in the basement with some guy. He was short and ugly, with curly dark hair and a stupid looking pencil moustache.

It was a lousy party and I was only there because my girlfriend had dumped me after two years and I'd needed to get out of the house.

"I have the best idea ever for a movie," the guy said.

"Uh-huh." The guy was drunk out of his mind.

"No, really man. It's true. The funny thing is, it'd only work as a movie. It wouldn't really work as a book or a TV show."

"Uh-huh," I said.

Then he told me his idea. It was a great idea. It couldn't miss.

"Jesus, that's not bad," I said. "Son of a bitch. That might be the best idea I've ever heard. How the fuck did you ever come up with that?"

He shrugged. "Ah man, you know. Sometimes shit just comes to you. They say everybody's got at least one story in them."

"Yeah, but I mean, Jesus. You should be careful who you tell. An idea that good, somebody'll steal it."

"I know. That's why I haven't pitched it to anybody. You're the first person I've told it to."

"Why me?" I said.

"You've got a face you can trust man," he said. He picked up a glass of gin off the coffee table, emptied it and passed out.

I thought about it. There was nobody else down there, so I bashed the guy's head in on the table. An idea like that's once in a lifetime. Not even. It was too good to pass up.

I tried to make it look like bad luck, like he'd just fallen off the couch the wrong way. It had the reek of alcohol and the whiff of plausibility.

I went upstairs and mingled for a bit. My whole body shook, but overall I managed to act pretty normal. I left around quarter after two. I didn't sleep at all.

I waited a week, because I was afraid it would look suspicious, and then I bought a ticket to LA. I tried to meet with a bunch of big producers, but they didn't know who I was, so they wouldn't see me.

After five days, I finally cornered an agent in a parking lot outside of a Denny's. It was after midnight and the lot was quiet. The guy wasn't much of a player, but he had a couple of clients that I'd heard of.

"Who the fuck are you man?" he said to me.

"I'm nobody yet, but I've got a brilliant idea for a movie. The best idea anyone's ever had. The best idea ever," I said.

"Yeah. You and everyone else."

"No. I'm serious. Trust me. You want to represent me on this."

He shrugged. "Alright. Let's hear it hotshot. Pitch it to me. But keep it brief. A hundred words or less."

I told him the idea, just like the guy on the couch had told me.

"Shit. That is a great fucking idea," the agent said. He leaned forward and put his hands on his knees and hyperventilated. "Jesus."

"So does that mean you're interested?"

"Definitely. Just hang on. Wait right here. I'll be two seconds," he said.

He walked across the parking lot. He pushed a button and a BMW started. The agent got into the BMW, backed it out and gunned it straight at me. I tried to dive out of the way, but I didn't make it. The grille crushed the left side of my skull.

The next thing I knew, I was sitting in the middle of a giant waiting room. I was on a leather couch that was in a square facing outwards. I couldn't see the ends of the room. It seemed to stretch on forever.

A woman walked by. She was about fifty, heavy set and frumpy. When she saw me, she stopped. She leaned down and took hold of my head.

"Tch. That's a nasty one," she said.

I reached up and felt my temple. There was a big divot and my hand came away sticky with blood.

"You must have just gotten here," the woman said.

"Yeah. I guess so. I'm starving. Is there somewhere around here I can get something to eat?"

"There's a vending machine right over there," she said.

I went and got a chocolate bar and a bag of chips from the vending machine and used up the last of my change. I sat back down on the couch and opened the chips. They were stale.

A guy came and sat down beside me. He was short and ugly and had dark curly hair and a pencil moustache.

"You remember me?" he said.

I looked at him carefully.

"Ho shit." That's when I figured out I was dead.

"That's right you son of a bitch. I'm the guy whose idea you stole and then you killed. You fucking beat my brains in on a coffee table. That's fucking sick. How can you live with yourself?"

"I'm dead." He threw me on the ground and my chips spilled everywhere. "That was my last buck," I said. He started kicking me. He was strong for a little guy. "Jesus. Ow, fuck, Jesus!"

"You fucking thief! You fucking thief! You stole my idea and then you fucking killed me!"

I'd killed him before I'd stolen his idea, but I decided not to quibble.

"I'm sorry," I said.

"You're sorry. Aw, he's sorry. Good for you. You're not forgiven."

He kept kicking me. I understood where he was coming from, but his kicks were sharp. I was probably bleeding internally. I wondered if I could die twice.

It went on for a while. The guy had incredible stamina. It ended when two other guys came along and pulled him off me. I caught my breath and tried to stand up, but my midsection hurt too much. I crawled as far as the couch and that was it.

"If it makes you feel any better, the guy I told your idea to ran me over with his car," I said.

He spat in my face and then he walked away.

I felt like shit for a couple of days afterwards. I mostly lay on my back on the couch. The fluorescent lights overhead made it hard to sleep, but at least I was able to eat and drink. The couch was a constant source of change for the vending machines. It was all different currencies, but the machines didn't seem to care. At one point, I pulled a handful of bronze coins with Tiberius' head on them. They were in mint condition. They would have been worth a fortune. The machine took five of them for a can of pop.

After two days of lying there, I got bored and went wandering. I decided I had to find the guy again and make it right. At least say sorry. Hopefully he wouldn't kick me this time.

While I was looking for him, I met a pretty woman who was about twenty.

"You're new here, aren't you?" she said.

I told her my story. I expected her to run away from me screaming, but she just shrugged.

"Don't feel too bad. That little shit had it coming. Nobody around here can stand him. He goes around telling everybody about this great idea as if it was his. A lot of people here had that same idea. Before he did. You'd be surprised," she said.

"I love you and I want to have sex with you. You're perfect," I said.

"Thanks. You're kind of cute, but that dent in the side of your head's not very attractive. Maybe when it heals."

We parted ways. I took to asking everybody I saw about the idea. They all seemed to know about it. Some people said it was this Chinese guy Chen-Yu who came up with it first, and some people said it was an Iranian woman named Masoumeh. They were both killed for the idea and they both blamed the other. But the most interesting story I heard was about a South African bushman who, one day, walked out of the desert and into a casino in Johannesburg and started talking. The only person who understood what he was saying was the croupier at the roulette wheel, a white man whose family had been there since before the Boer War.

The croupier killed the bushman in the alley behind the casino. He quit his job and wrote the screenplay. He put it in an envelope and addressed it to Hollywood, but the postman was curious and he opened the envelope. He went and killed the croupier and set to retyping the screenplay with his own name on it.

That was in nineteen thirty-seven. The screenplay never got to Hollywood, because the postman burned in a suspicious fire, along with both copies of the script.

As near as I can tell, everyone who ever had the idea told it to somebody else and then got murdered. I decided that when I found that ugly little shit and his pencil moustache I'd let him have it, the lying prick. It took me three days to find him.

"I'm sorry," I said, and then he kicked the shit out of me for half an hour.

I run into him from time to time and it always goes the same way. I say I'm sorry and he kicks the shit out of me for half an hour.

It's not all bad here, though. My head is healed and the perfect twenty year old woman had sex with me. She told me there's a new guy here. I haven't run across him yet, but it sounds like the new guy is the agent who ran me over.

The rumour going around now is that Clint Eastwood's making the idea into a movie. The guy's over eighty, but nobody dares to try and kill him.

About the Author
Andrew J Simpson was born and raised in Ottawa and lives in Toronto. His stories have appeared in journals both in Canada and internationally. He was awarded the Nicholas Hoare Prize for Short Fiction in 2005. His first anthology The Big Picture was published by BareBackPress in 2013. For more information on what he is doing check out versustheneanderthals.com.

Mechanical Heart
Melissa June

Falling droplets of my inner tears
saturating wheels as they slowly spin
tinged brown, my hearts rusted gears
the corroding metal that turns within

Where minutes pass, can't be saved
as blood is clotting within my veins
the dial of dying love is engraved
onto my heart, where time reins

Stopping my pulse, as hands stilled
the vessels of cerise blood drain
while chambers are vastly filled
with tear drops of my unwinding pain

Drowning the bearings, you tore apart
I murmur loves ticking sound
sink the key, to my mechanical heart
to never again be so blindly wound.

Malfunctioning Lover
Melissa June

Entangled within you're distorted chains
your pendulum swinging in reverse
as the spring of our love strains
from weights that made us disperse

As you're painfully inaccurate hands
tick vigorously through my life
I cry my last tear drop as it lands
upon uplifting hope, freedoms knife

Dauntlessly cutting wires to unravel
from a future that seems unstable
untangling to allow my heart to travel
faraway, free from you're love's fable

Reminiscing the times forever glassed
within your soul, beneath eyes so bleak
I lock the door to my defective past
as I unwind the chime, of my beloved antique.

About the Author:
Melissa June is a twenty five year old poetess from Windsor Ontario, Canada. She has always had a passion for writing. She enjoys writing poems that are metaphorical, poems of fantasy, loneliness, and poems of love to name a few. Her dreams are to one day publish a poetry book and being a mother of three beautiful girls she hopes to touch more upon children's poems and to create children's rhyming books.

As the Moon is to You
Teresa Di Matteo

I borrowed the moon
for such a short amount
of time,
you did not
even notice
it was missing,
and I held it in
my hands,
the way you would
hold it in your pocket ---
I sang to it
a lullaby
for all of the many nights
you had yelled at it,
and in our humble visit,
the moon and I,
we danced,
and we laughed
at you
for pity's sake,
that it would cover you
in shadow
the way you had cloaked
the night
with your heavy laden self,
always blaming the moon
for being brightest
in the sky,
for being the light
in my eyes,
such a glorious companion,
when you knew, all along,
you could have been so too.

Nostalgia
Teresa Di Matteo

When we were young
we scraped our knees
and it felt good.
We looked to the street
lamps like golden lanterns
to light our way home,
as luminaries with promises
of warm blankets
and sweet delights,
and for that, we knew
when the day had ended,
when our breath finally
caught up with us,
for we were certainly
more inclined to hold
warm hands and
turn over our beds
while our hair clung
to sheets of perfumed lilac,
the last trace of warm weather,
and covering our eyes to
hide from the harvest moon,
we laughed ourselves
to sleep through thin walls
of in-jokes and outcomes.

About the Author:
Teresa Di Matteo is a writer of poetry and prose. She has written editorials for indiemusicreviewer,com and contributed poetry to Tuck Magazine. In her spare time, she can be found playing folk tunes on her twelve string guitar, or blogging on her website teaatwoodrows.com.

The Learning Channel

WARNING: Lengthy exposure to this oversaturated slew of reality based programming may cause severe loss of self-respect, IQ points, feelings of self-loathing and overeating. Consult your physician if you have a redneck, Honey Boo Boo thighs, or if you have an urge to boss around cakes and other pastries.

Matryoshka
Peter Jelen

I am black. My world is white. My world is a figment of someone's imagination. I am a figment of someone's imagination. I do not know whose imagination created me, I do not know what this imagination wants from me, I only know what He has allowed me to know, and He has allowed me to know this:

There is something else beyond the covers of my world. There is something else beyond its spine. There is something more outside of these pages.

When the Imagination makes me look out of my window I see a fountain, and a garden, and a tall brick wall with barbed wire covering its ledge like curly gray hair. I see that, but that's not what's really there, what's really there, is a white page, with the words:

`When Albert Overton looks out of his window he sees a fountain, and a garden, and a tall brick wall with barbed wire covering its ledge like curly gray hair.`

Some of the letters in my world will wear the word uniform. Some will wear the words `suit and tie`. I wear the words `white gown`.

The letters wearing suits and ties try to convince me that there is nothing else beyond the covers of our world. They try to convince me that "there is no cover," that "there is no spine." They try to convince me that I am not letters, that they are not letters. They try to tell me that I am a human being, that my name is Albert Overton.

"Look at yourself," the Imagination will make them say, "can't you see Albert, you have two legs, and two hands; you have a body. You're not letters. You're not the alphabet."

"If I am not the alphabet," He'll make me say, "if you're not the alphabet, then how come we're trapped in this book?"

"We're not trapped in a book, Albert. It's a figment of your imagination."

"Wrong! We're a figment of *the* Imagination. Can't you feel it? We're moving towards the climax. Action is rising. Tensions are building. We're about to hit the critical incident!"

"What will happen at the critical incident?"

"I don't know! That's why I'm scared."

"But if you don't really exist, if our world, like you say, is only a figment of an imagination, why are you so scared?"

"I still feel. My feelings may not be real, but I still feel them."

"Do you think you're the main character in the story?"

"I don't know. He won't let me know that much. Maybe we're all main characters.

Maybe we all have our own stories. Maybe the stories have already been written, and we're all just resting beside one another on an astral bookshelf waiting to be read."

"Who will read us?"

"Whoever's reading us right now."

"Are they letters too?"

"I knew you'd say that!"

"How did you know?"

"It was obvious our dialogue was going in that direction."

"Dialogue?"

"Haven't you noticed that everything we say seems contrived? How every sentence blends in with the next and advances the plot."

"I'm not quite following you, Albert."

"Watch. Ask me a question, any question, and I guarantee that it will advance the plot in some way."

"Alright. How have you and your wife been getting along?"

"Fine."

"So, how did that advance the plot?"

"It gave Him the perfect lead in."

"Lead in to what?"

"For me to tell the reader about my wife."

The Imagination named my wife Barbara. He named my two sons Philip and Simon. He made Barbara have soft red hair and a voluptuous figure that resembled the letter X. He made her voice sound sugary and pacifying. He made us meet in university. He made me bump into her at the campus bookstore. He made her drop her books. He made me pick them up, and when our eyes met, He made us fall in love. He planned the wedding for October, six months after our graduation and made us stay married ever since.

When the Imagination sends Barbara to visit me, He makes her bring up old times, the times we had before He let me find out about Him.

"Remember our wedding, Albert?" He'll make Barbara say.

"Our wedding was half a sentence. It meant nothing in the big picture. He was simply building character."

"Stop talking like that!"

"It's part of the plot."

"There is no plot!"

"You'll see, if He decides to incorporate you into the critical incident, you'll see. You'll see what He has planned for me."

"I wish you never would've taken that promotion. That's what did this to you, the stress."

"I had to take that job. It couldn't have happened any other way. It was the perfect set up. And now this is the perfect set up."

"Set up for what?"

"For me to tell the reader about how I found out about Him."

The Imagination plotted the story, my imaginary life, quite ingeniously. He made the first thirty-five years pass by without a hint of His existence. He did, however, plant seeds along the way. And when His seeds had grown, and the flowers bloomed, He picked them, and tied a perfect red ribbon around them.

I know that, because He has let me smell the flowers. He sent them to me in the mail. He sent them in the form of a manuscript. He made one of my assistants rush into to my office and say, "Boss, you godda read this."

"What is it?"

"Spooky. Really spooky. I couldn't get past the first few pages. It was creeping me out."

"Give it here, I'll take a look at it."

The Imagination made me pour a cup of coffee and plop myself down in my soft chair. He made me brush away the stacks of unread, never-will-be read manuscripts off of my desk, and skim over the cover-page:

Matryoshka

I wasn't sure what that meant, so I buzzed my assistant, "Hey Ronnie?" He made me say, "What's Matryoshka?"

"It's those wooden dolls. You know, where you open one up, and there's another one inside, and another one inside of that one, and so on."

"I thought so."

"Have you started reading?"

"Not yet, why do you ask?"

"You'll see."

I linked my fingers together and stretched out my arms. "All right," He made me mutter to myself, "here we go." I licked the tip of my finger and turned over the cover page. I read the first paragraph nearly a dozen times with my jaw unlocked and my mouth hanging open, adjusting my glasses, unable to believe what I was reading.

"Ha, ha, ha," He made me chuckle sarcastically as I buzzed Ronnie, "very funny."

"What?"

"Your phony manuscript. Was it you or Dave?"

"Was it me or Dave what? It came in the mail. You think Dave wrote it?"

"He must have."

"Are you still gunna read it?"

"I'll skim it over."

And so I did, and I couldn't put it down. The more I read the more my stomach began to turn. The more I read the more confused and distorted my thoughts became; the more I wanted to peel off my skin and find out if I was really alive. By the fourth chapter I knew without a hint of doubt that Dave hadn't written the manuscript. I knew it wasn't a coincidence. I knew the character in the manuscript was me, that the life being described in the manuscript was mine. I knew, by the time I finished the book, and stumbled out of my office, that I was trapped in a book, and so did the Albert on Paper.

Albert on Paper, the main character in the manuscript, was also an editor at Ulysses Publishing. He was also said to read every half-decent manuscript that made it past his assistants. He also had a wife named Barbara with soft red hair and a voluptuous figure that resembled the letter X. They too had met in university, when Albert bumped into her at the campus bookstore. And just like me, all of that changed for Albert on Paper when his assistant Ronnie rushed into his office and said, "Boss, you godda read this."

I must have read that line fifty times. I had no thoughts as I read it, and reread it, I just kept reading it, and reading it, and reading it until the words had lost all meaning. The Imagination had not equipped me with the mental capacity to interpret what was happening. He did, however, endow me with the overriding urge to crumple up the manuscript, set it on fire, and throw it out the window. He had given me the urge, but he wouldn't let me do that. Instead He made me read on. Read about Albert pouring himself a cup of coffee, buzzing his assistant, and saying, "Hey Ronnie, what's Matryoshka?"

And just like I had, Albert on Paper linked his fingers together, stretched out his arms and muttered to himself, "All right, here we go."

And just like me, Albert on Paper read:

```
Albert Overton is black. His world is white.
His  world  is  a  figment  of  someone's
imagination.  He  is  a  figment  of  someone's
imagination. He does not know whose imagination
created  him,  he  does  not  know  what  this
```

imagination wants from him, he only knows what he has been allowed him to know. And he has been allowed to know this: There is something else beyond the covers of his world. There is something else beyond its spine. There is something more outside of its pages.

Albert on Paper couldn't believe it. His jaw unlocked. His mouth fell open. He thought it was one of his assistants playing a joke on him. Chuckling sarcastically, he buzzed Ronnie and said, "Ha, ha, ha, very funny."

But Ronnie assured him it was no joke, it came in the mail.

"Are you still gunna read it?"

"I'll skim it over."

And so he did.

Albert on Paper sat in his chair shaking, trembling, unable to read fast enough. The more he read the more his stomach began to turn. The more he read the more confused and distorted his thoughts became; the more he wanted to peel off his skin and find out if he was really alive. By the time Albert reached the fourth chapter, he knew, without a hint of doubt, that his assistant wasn't playing a joke. That this was no coincidence.

The manuscript Albert on Paper was reading really got interesting when Albert the Character's assistant Ronnie rushed into his office and said, "Boss, you godda read this."

And just like us, Albert the Character poured a cup of coffee and plopped himself down in front of his desk. And just like us he read over the cover page, and was unsure what the title meant, and just like us he buzzed his assistant, and asked, "Hey Ronnie, what's Matryoshka?"

By the time I reached that point in the manuscript I was crippled by fear. So was Albert on Paper, and so was Albert the Character. We couldn't believe, nor understand what was happening, or how it was happening. We pulled our eyes away from our manuscripts and gave our heads a shake. As we cautiously gazed around our offices trying to comprehend this physical manifestation of a fictional world we felt as if a film was being removed from our retinas and we were looking at everything under a microscope. Only our world wasn't composed of atoms and molecules and cells, it was composed of letters. Letters upon letters. I thought it was an illusion, a stress-induced hallucination. So did Albert on Paper. So did Albert the Character. Our desks, the books on our shelves, the buildings outside our windows, they'd all lost their form and mutated into type. We no longer saw a wooden desk beneath us. We only saw the words: `wooden desk` beneath us.

Our manuscripts had also changed. They were no longer made of paper, but of the word paper. We read faster and faster trying to get to the end. We read faster and faster trying to understand what was happening to us, wanting to know what was going to happen to us. The tension built. The action rose. We hit the critical incident and the manuscript concluded when Albert the Character suddenly shot up from his desk, stumbled out into the hall, and bumped into his assistant Ronnie, who asked him, "Was it any good, Boss?"

At that moment, Albert on Paper suddenly shot up from his desk, stumbled out into the hall, and bumped into his assistant Ronnie, who asked him, "Was it any good, Boss?"

And that's where the manuscript ended for me, and that's when I suddenly shot up from my desk, stumbled out into the hall, bumped into my assistant Ronnie, and he asked me, "Was it any good, Boss?"

About the Author:

Peter Jelen has spent the last six years living and working in Japan, China, and South Korea, where he currently calls home. In 2012 he published his first collection of short stories Better Than God though BareBackPress. Check his art out on www.peterjelen.com.

Acknowledgements:

Thank you to all of the writers whose creativity, passion, and emails made this book possible. Your work is all appreciated and this anthology is proof of that. Special thanks to Mike Algera for working so expediently and meticulously throughout the editing process.

Old Gods for New
Mike Algera

At a sidewalk sale
you will meet a dealer
he will tell you
he has monuments of old gods
for sale, "Pick a God,
and worship however you please."   ~ Excerpt from Old Gods for New

Old Gods for New reflects upon personal triumphs and demons, love and longing, the past and never-was; musings that spark both the artistry of playful banter as well as lyrical madness. Writing that is quirky yet daring, combining scratch words into something new.

$19.99
138 Pages
6" x 9"
ISBN-13: 978-0988075078
BISAC: Poetry/ General

Little Human Accidents:
Damon Ferrell Marbut

Damon Ferrell Marbut devastates the notion of apology in poetry with a tender recklessness in *Little Human Accidents*, poems that examine a personal evolution of sexuality and identity while treating the unavoidable step towards adulthood like a punching bag, especially in his free flowing self reflexive poems like *Mornings Like This* and *So What*.

$19.99
150 pages
6" x 9"
ISBN 13: 978-0988075092
BISAC: Poetry/ General

The Big Picture
Andrew J. Simpson

I WALKED UP BEHIND GOD AND STUCK A SIGN ON HIS BACK. IT SAID "FREE WILL," OR "KICK ME."

The government is taxing your dreams and moments are being captured and held against their will. Murphy's Law is suspended pending the outcome of a constitutional challenge; a best-selling author writes and publishes the same novel fifteen times without anyone catching on, and all of humanity is put into receivership over a missing cup of coffee.

$18.99
240pages
6" x 9"
ISBN-13: 978-0992035501
BISAC: Fiction / General

Words that Burn
Wayne F. Burke

BEWARE: Wayne F. Burke and his Words that Burn is not only poetry, its arson. A combustible collection of poetry that will fry anyone's imagination: jails, arrests, a bad childhood, and life in the raw. Words that Burn is a brutally honest evisceration of one man's experience of life on this planet written with verve and the unadorned yet eloquent language of where the poet came from.

$18.99
132pages
6" x 9"
ISBN-13: 978-0992035518
BISAC: Poetry / General

www.barebackpress.com

www.ingramcontent.com/pod-product-compliance
Lightning Source LLC
Chambersburg PA
CBHW072357020726
47506CB00004B/1152